# 大学基础英语教程 ②

## 教师用书

总主编　张敬源

主　编　晋胜利　郭平建
副主编　邵　荣　侯文忠　王　茹
编　者　晋　红　李润娥　王亚丽　赵宇霞
　　　　郭　佳　梁旭红　李正娜　李砚霞
　　　　高卉阳　闫美荣　张雪梅
审　订　Margaret Fawcett

图书在版编目(CIP)数据

大学基础英语教程(2)教师用书/晋胜利,郭平建主编. —北京:北京大学出版社,2008.11
(面向新世纪的立体化网络化英语学科建设丛书)
ISBN 978-7-301-14365-0

Ⅰ.大… Ⅱ.①晋…②郭… Ⅲ.英语—高等学校—教学参考资料 Ⅳ.H31

中国版本图书馆CIP数据核字(2008)第163095号

| | |
|---|---|
| 书　　　名: | 大学基础英语教程（2）教师用书 |
| 著作责任者: | 晋胜利　郭平建　主编 |
| 策　　　划: | 张　冰　高生文　张建民 |
| 责任编辑: | 张建民 |
| 标准书号: | ISBN 978-7-301-14365-0/H·2085 |
| 出版发行: | 北京大学出版社 |
| 地　　　址: | 北京市海淀区成府路205号　100871 |
| 网　　　址: | http://www.pup.cn |
| 电　　　话: | 邮购部 62752015　发行部 62750672　编辑部 62755217　出版部 62754962 |
| 电子邮箱: | zbing@pup.pku.edu.cn |
| 印　刷　者: | 北京飞达印刷有限责任公司 |
| 经　销　者: | 新华书店 |
| | 787毫米×1092毫米　16开本　10.75印张　270千字 |
| | 2008年11月第1版　2008年11月第1次印刷 |
| 定　　　价: | 25.00元（配有光盘） |

未经许可,不得以任何方式复制或抄袭本书之部分或全部内容。
版权所有,侵权必究　举报电话: 010-62752024
电子邮箱: fd@pup.pku.edu.cn

# 前　言

教育部《大学英语课程教学要求》(以下简称《教学要求》)明确指出:"我国幅员辽阔,各地区、各高校之间情况差异较大,大学英语教学应按照分类指导、因材施教的原则,以适应个性化教学的实际需要。"

《大学基础英语教程》即是依据《教学要求》编写的一套大学英语教材,主要适用于全国各高等院校艺术、体育类学生,民族地区学生和其他一些大学入学时英语基础相对薄弱的非英语专业大学生,旨在使学生通过本教材的系统学习,在英语语言知识、应用技能、学习策略和跨文化交际方面能够达到《教学要求》中规定的高等学校非英语专业本科毕业生应达到的基本要求。

## 一、编写原则

《大学基础英语教程》在编写过程中力图体现以下编写原则:

1. 以《教学要求》为依据,重点培养学生英语综合应用能力。
2. 以人为本,因人制宜,始终考虑适用对象的现有英语水平和实际学习需求。
3. 旨在使学生通过本教材的学习,做到学有所用、学以致用、以用促学、学用统一。力争使语言知识的传授与语言运用能力的提高做到相辅相成、有机互补,既不片面强调语言知识的传授,也不片面强调没有坚实基础的语言能力的提高。

## 二、教材特色

与国内其他大学英语优秀教材相比,本教程的特色主要体现为"唯实"、"简约"、"实用"、"教育"四个方面。洞察适用对象外语水平和学习需求之实并以之为本,教材编著与设计力求因应适用对象之求并扼之以要,高度重视学生综合文化素养的培养以及所学外语知识和技能的实际应用,寓人文素养与道德教育于外语学习的潜移默化之中。具体体现如下:

### 1. 唯实性

本教材专门为全国各高校艺术、体育类学生,民族地区学生和其他一些大学入学时英语基础相对薄弱的非英语专业大学生所编写,编写体例、课文选材、练习设计等均体现了较强的针对性,以提高学生综合运用语言的能力为出发点和最终归宿,针对学生的薄弱环节和实际需要,做到因应需求、有的放矢。

### 2. 简约性

与国内现有其他优秀教材相比，本教材依据目标学生实际情况，不求教材大而全，突出其简约而实用的特点。同时，本教材编写融听、说、读、写、译多种语言技能培养为一体，各册既各有侧重，又有机相连，从而达到全面培养学生综合运用英语能力的目标。

### 3. 实用性

本教材选材力求语言规范、严谨，选文力求与适用对象的专业和兴趣相关，同时知识性与趣味性兼备。选文富于思想内涵，融语言、文化、技能为一体，有助于学生运用所学外语知识就课文涉及的相关问题阐述自己的观点和看法。这不仅能训练学生的语言技能，同时也能培养学生的综合素养。重点语言知识及技能讲解以及练习的编配侧重使学生学以致用，在知识运用中检验知识，弥补不足。

### 4. 教育性

外语学习不仅事关学生综合运用英语的能力和学生的国际视野，更是人才培养的有机组成部分。本教材选文不仅注重激发学生的学习兴趣，培养学生的外语技能，更加注重学生综合人文素养的提升和积极人生观与正确价值观的培养，使之在潜移默化之中，启迪学生的思想，陶冶学生的情操。

## 三、内容结构

《大学基础英语教程》供高等院校非英语专业本科生两学年4个学期使用，重点培养学生综合运用所学英语知识和技能，有效进行口语及书面交际的能力，提高其综合外语文化素养。全教程共4册，每册供一个学期使用。每册教材含12单元课文和3套单元自测题。每一单元含相同或相关主题主、副课文各一篇。主课文前有本单元内容简介 (Preview)、听力活动 (Lead-in Listening)、口语活动 (Communicative Activity)。主课文由读前问题 (Pre-reading Questions)、课文 (Text)、生词(New Words)、词组(Phrases and Expressions)、专有名词(Proper Names)、注释(Notes)、练习(Exercises)几个部分组成。每篇主课文后均配有课文理解(Getting the Message)、词汇学习(Developing Your Vocabulary)、要点综述(Recognizing Main Ideas)、英汉互译(Trying the Translation)、语篇构建(Organizing Your Ideas)和话题讨论(Beyond the Reading) 6项练习。副课文后同样附有生词、词组和注释，配有课文理解(题型与大学英语四级考试速读部分相同)和要点综述两项练习。每单元还配有重点知识或技能(Skill in Focus)及相关练习(Exercises)。

每册书含3个单元自测题，分别插入第4、第8、第12单元之后，自测题内容是对相关单元重点知识与内容的复习与检测，以相关单元内容检测为主，辅之以其他能力测试题。题型与大学英语四级考试新题型以及全国公共英语等级考试（PETS）相近或相同。

每单元可安排4学时，教师可视课文的长度、难度及各校学生的具体情况适度调节。

教师参考书中配有每篇课文的参考译文、背景知识、难点分析与练习答案，重点练习部分附有练习答案详解，供教师备课时参考使用。

4册教材以一所学校为主，由几所学校合作完成，采用大体相同编写体例，各册既各有侧重，自成一体，又有机相连。专项知识和技能部分重在技能训练，4册教材分别侧重关键语法、阅读技能、翻译技巧、写作训练。

《大学基础英语教程》第一册由北京科技大学彭漪教授、何伟博士／博士后主编；第二册由山西长治学院晋胜利教授、北京服装学院郭平建教授主编；第三册由华中科技大学许明武教授主编；第四册由北京交通大学蒋学清教授主编。每册书均由一名资深外籍专家审定，以确保教材内容及语言的规范性、严谨性、自然性与真实性。

限于编者水平，疏漏与错讹之处在所难免，敬请专家、读者批评指正。

编者
2008年5月

# Contents

**Unit One**  **Unspoken Love** ............................................................ 1
    Text A    Me, in Concert ............................................................ 2
    Text B    A Prodigy's Early Years ............................................ 7
    Reading in Focus    英语阅读的瓶颈—词汇多义性 ............ 12

**Unit Two**  **Championship** ............................................................ 13
    Text A    A Dream Comes True ............................................ 14
    Text B    Real Champions ...................................................... 20
    Reading in Focus    英语长、难句的阅读(1) ................ 24

**Unit Three**  **Life in Art** ............................................................ 25
    Text A    Clay Figurines .......................................................... 26
    Text B    New Year's Wood Block Paintings ........................ 30
    Reading in Focus    英语长、难句的阅读(2) ................ 35

**Unit Four**  **Hip-hop Culture** ...................................................... 39
    Text A    Not Merely Music: The Phenomenon of Hip-hop ...... 40
    Text B    What Is Hip-hop to Me ............................................ 45
    Reading in Focus    英语长、难句的阅读(3) ................ 53

**Keys to Test One** ................................................................ 55

**Unit Five**  **Never Give Up** ........................................................ 58
    Text A    Heart of Gold .......................................................... 59
    Text B    Run, Patti, Run! ...................................................... 64
    Reading in Focus    分词表示的逻辑关系 ...................... 68

**Unit Six**  **City Symbol** ............................................................ 69
    Text A    The Statue of Liberty—A Diplomatic Gift .......... 70
    Text B    The Manneken Pis .................................................. 76
    Reading in Focus    连词—意义承接的纽带 ................ 81

**Unit Seven**  **Ultimate Challenge** ................................................ 83
    Text A    Bungee Jumping .................................................... 84
    Text B    Rock Climbing ........................................................ 90
    Reading in Focus    识别主题句 .................................... 95

# Contents

**Unit Eight    Stagecraft** ......................................................... **96**
    Text A    Beijing Opera ............................................. 97
    Text B    Facial Makeups ......................................... 103
    Reading in Focus    阅读特定信息—定义 ................ 107

**Keys to Test Two** ................................................................. **111**

**Unit Nine    Sports in China** ............................................... **114**
    Text A    Sports in China ......................................... 115
    Text B    Football Games of Old China ................... 119
    Reading in Focus    英语阅读猜词技巧 .................... 123

**Unit Ten    Cartoon Stars** .................................................. **126**
    Text A    Creation of Stars ....................................... 127
    Text B    Barbie Doll's Mom-Ruth Handler ............. 132
    Reading in Focus    指代一致—英语阅读的逻辑连贯 ... 135

**Unit Eleven    Power of Music** ........................................... **139**
    Text A    Keep on Singing ....................................... 140
    Text B    Music Has Power ..................................... 145
    Reading in Focus    英语句子中的省略 .................... 149

**Unit Twelve    Fans Forever** .............................................. **150**
    Text A    World Cup Dad ......................................... 151
    Text B    Roger Maris and Me ................................. 156
    Reading in Focus    语篇中概括句的识别 ................ 160

**Keys to Test Three** .............................................................. **161**

# Unspoken Love

## Script for Lead-in Listening

Listen to the following conversation and fill in the blanks with the correct words or phrases. You may choose the words or phrases from the list given.

**Larry:** Hello, Sally, I'd like to ask you to go to a concert with me this evening. Could you?
**Sally:** Thanks for asking. But I have to finish my paper first.
**Larry:** Then what about tomorrow evening? I'm sure you'd enjoy the symphony concert at the National Concert Hall.
**Sally:** Tomorrow evening suits me just fine.
**Larry:** It's a new concert hall.
(During the intermission)
**Larry:** Would you like to stretch your legs?
**Sally:** Sure.
**Larry:** Let's get a soft drink.
**Sally:** Do we have time?
**Larry:** We've got fifteen minutes. That's enough.
**Sally:** The seats are excellent. We're right in the center.
**Larry:** Is this the first time you've come to a symphony concert?
**Sally:** No. I've been to concerts a couple of times with my parents.
**Larry:** Do you have large concert halls in your city?
**Sally:** We have two. One is like this one. The other is a little smaller.
**Larry:** That's great. Well, we'd better get back to our seats. It's about to start.

## WORDS AND EXPRESSIONS IN LEAD-IN LISTENING

**symphony** *n.* a long complicated piece of music for a large orchestra, in three or four main parts
  *Beethoven's Fifth Symphony is my favorite.*

**suit** *v.* to be convenient or useful to sb
  *If we meet at 2, would that suit you?*

**stretch one's legs** (*informal*) to go for a short walk after sitting for some time
  *It was good to get out of the car and stretch our legs.*

**soft drink** a cold drink that does not contain alcohol
  *Wait here, I'll get some soft drink for you.*

Encourage your students to recall some words related to music, such as March, orchestra, notes, half note, quarter note, musical notation, staff, symphony concert, concert hall and so on.

## ME, IN CONCERT

## Background Information

1. **Minuet**   (from French menu: "small") The elegant couple dance that dominated aristocratic European ballrooms, especially in France and England, from c. 1650 to c. 1750. Reputedly derived from the French folk dance branle de Poitou,  the court minuet used smaller steps and became slower and increasingly etiquette-laden and spectacular. Dancers, in the order of their social position,  often performed versions with especially choreographed figures,  or floor patterns,  and prefaced the dance with stylized bows and curtsies to partners and spectators. The basic floor pattern outlined by the dancers was at first a figure 8 and, later, the letter Z.
2. **Chord**   In music, three or more single pitches heard simultaneously. Depending on the harmonic style, chords may be consonant, implying repose, or dissonant, implying subsequent resolution to and by another chord.  In traditional Western harmony,  chords are formed by super-impositions of intervals of a third.

## Language Points

1. **gleam**   *v.*   to shine with a pale clear light
   *His teeth gleamed under his moustache.*
   *He laughed, his eyes gleaming with amusement.*
2. **hum**   *v.*   (informal) to be full of activity
   *By nine o'clock, the restaurant was humming.*
   *The streets were humming with life.*
   **hum to oneself**   to sing a tune by making a continuous sound with one's lips closed
   *Tony was humming to himself as he drove along.*
3. **off and on/on and off**   from time to time, now and again
   *We've been going out together for five years, off and on.*
   *It rained on and off all day.*
4. **remind sb about/of sth/to do sth**   to help sb remember sth important
   *That song always reminds me of our first date.*
   *Remind me to buy some milk tonight.*

The girls constantly had to be reminded about their chores.

**remind sb (of) what/how, etc.**

I was reminded how lucky I was.

5. **timid** *adj.* shy and nervous, not brave

He stopped in the doorway, too timid to go in.

They've been rather timid in the changes they've made.

6. **not much of a...** not a good ...

He is not much of a tennis player.

I'm not much of a dancer, I'm afraid.

It wasn't really much of a storm.

7. **defective** *adj.* having a fault or faults, not perfect or complete

Her hearing was found to be slightly defective.

The disease is caused by a defective gene.

**defect** *n.* a fault or a lack of something that means that something or someone is not perfect

All the cars are tested for defects before they leave the factory.

8. **dwindle (away)** *n.* to become gradually less or smaller

The elephant population is dwindling.

His money had dwindled away.

9. **float** *v.* to move slowly on water or in the air

I looked up at the clouds floating in the sky.

Leaves floated gently down from the trees.

The sound of her voice came floating down from an upstairs window.

10. **poise** *v.* to be or hold sth steady in a particular position, especially above sth else

He poised the bottle over her glass, "More wine?"

She poised the javelin in her hand before the throw.

He was poising himself to launch a final attack.

*n.* a calm, confident way of behaving

Louisa seems to have much more poise and confidence.

11. **torture** *n.* (informal) mental or physical suffering; sth that causes this

The waiting must be torture for you.

The interview was sheer torture from start to finish.

*v.* a. to hurt sb physically or mentally

b. to make sb feel extremely unhappy or anxious

Many of the rebels were captured and tortured by secret police.

He spent his life tortured by the memories of his childhood.

12. **inspire** *v.* to give sb the desire, confidence or enthusiasm to do sth well

I hope this success will inspire you to greater efforts.

Inspired by the sunny weather, I decided to explore the woods.

**inspire sb to do sth**

He inspired many young people to take up the sport.

13. **hang (on) in there**  (*imformal*) to continue doing sth in different circumstances

   *Don't worry. Just hang on in there.*

   **hang on**   to hold sth tightly

   *She hung on to the side of the cart as it rattled over the stones.*
   *Hang on tight!*

   **hang on!** (*British English spoken*)

   a. used to ask or tell someone to wait

      *Hang on! I can't keep up with you.*

   b. used when you have just noticed or thought of something that is interesting or wrong

      *Hang on! I think that movie is fantastic.*

14. **on earth**   used after negative nouns or pronouns to emphasize what is saying

   *Nothing on earth would persuade me to go with him.*
   *What on earth do you mean?*
   *Why on earth did you take the dog into the churchyard?*
   *How on earth could all this be explained?*

15. **focus on**   to give attention, effort, etc. to

   *All eyes focused on her.*
   *She turned the camera and focused on Martin's face.*

   **focus sth on sth**

   *He focused his binoculars on the building opposite.*

   **focus your attention/mind/efforts on sth**

   *She tried to focus her mind on her work.*

16. **command**   *v.*   to control

   *The party that commands a majority of seats in Parliament forms the government.*
   *The party was no longer able to command a majority in Parliament.*

   *n.*   control and authority over a situation or a group of people

   **in command (of sth)**

   *Lieutenant Peters was now in command.*
   *He felt fully in command of the situation.*

   **take command (of sth)**  begin controlling a group or situation and making decisions

   *The fire officer took command, ordering everyone to leave the building.*

   **at one's command**

   *Each congressman has a large staff at his command (=available to be used).*

17. **thrill**   *v.*   to excite or please sb very much

   *His music continues to thrill audiences.*
   *In the 1960s, the public thrilled to the idea of space exploration.*

   *n.* [C]   a sudden strong feeling of excitement and pleasure

   *Winning first place must have been quite a thrill.*
   *Even though I've been acting for years, I still get a thrill out of going on stage.*

18. **give up**   to stop trying to do sth

*Darren has decided to give up football at the end of this season.*

*She gave up her job and started writing poetry.*

**give up doing sth**

*I gave up trying to persuade him to continue with his studies.*

**give oneself up**   to allow yourself or someone else to be caught by the police or enemy soldiers

*The siege ended peacefully after the gunman gave himself up.*

**give sb up to**

*In the end, his family gave him up to the police.*

# Answer Keys

## I. Getting the Message
1. B    2. C    3. A    4. D    5. C

## II. Developing Your Vocabulary
### Section A
1. gleamed   2. thrilled   3. defect   4. applaud   5. commands   6. dwindled

### Section B
1. focused on       2. on and off/off and on       3. much of a
4. remind...of      5. give up                     6. hang in there

## III. Recognizing Main Ideas
1. nervous       2. performing      3. keep at      4. join
5. simple        6. practice        7. made         8. courage

## IV. Trying the Translation
### Section A
1. 学生们等待着登台演奏，紧张的气氛在空气中弥漫。
2. 出售旧钢琴，适合初学者使用，价格100元。
3. 这台钢琴的十几个琴键都有毛病，但主要琴键依然基本完好。
4. 我希望孩子能拥有的勇气如今使我挺起胸膛，手指在琴键上自由飘动。
5. 学到的是音乐还是勇气，哪一个更多一些，我难以确定。

### Section B
1. All the pianos look alike.
2. I am the right age for these computer courses.

3. Focus on the music book and practice this piece over and over.
4. I was watching a football match when I heard the knock.
5. My task is to finish the paper by Friday.

## V. Organizing Your Ideas

f a d e c b

参考译文

## 我在音乐会上演奏

不久前,我来到十几个孩子之中,家长们围在闪亮的钢琴周围。学生们等待着登台演奏,紧张的气氛在空气中弥漫。我也很紧张。我希望我的孩子们能有良好的表现。今天,平生头一次我也要亲自表演。

我从5岁起断断续续地上过一些音乐课。母亲厌倦了总要提醒我练习,让我终止了钢琴学习,我很胆怯,没有参加过演出,但音乐始终伴随着我的生活。

有一天,我看到了这样一则广告:"出售旧钢琴,适合初学者使用,价格100元。"我的女儿们正是学钢琴的年龄。我把孩子们塞进货车里,去看这台钢琴。

一百元似乎买不到一台像样的钢琴,这台钢琴的十几个琴键都有毛病,但主要琴键依然基本完好,至少对我这样没有受过训练的人来说它的音质还不错。

起初,孩子们学习钢琴的热情高涨。但一年不到的时间里,她们练习得越来越少,后来几乎中止。

我听到她们说:"我讨厌理论课。""我听不懂,太郁闷了。""我为什么非要上钢琴课?"我告诉女儿们她们必须完成这一年的学习,给自己一个机会。

你能想到她们的回答吗?"你要是很想弹钢琴的话就应该自己去学钢琴。"

我想了想。为什么不呢?我想象自己的手毫不费力地从琴键上滑过。

然而一旦开始学习,我的手就变成了准备敲击键盘的爪子。所有的琴键看起来都一个模样。女儿们心满意足地看着我折腾。我想她们喜欢听我演奏难听的和音、听我抱怨和道歉:"我承认我练习不够;我还没有准备好;我手腕伤了;狗把我的乐谱吃了。"

这是一件艰苦的活,和孩子们一同受折磨可以帮助她们坚持得长久一些。

在音乐会上,我的大女儿斯蒂芬妮坐在了钢琴旁,当她的手指滑过琴键时,我的脉搏加快,我屏住了呼吸。然后是我的小女儿。

接下来就轮到了我。我走到钢琴旁,用颤抖的手指打开乐谱。"我为什么要学钢琴呢?"我把注意力集中在那一页乐谱上。G小调小步舞曲是我反复练习过的曲目。我希望孩子能拥有的勇气如今使我挺起胸膛,手指在琴键上自由飘动……

我站起身来,双膝发软,走向座位时我听到了掌声。

我最小的女儿明年要学钢琴了,我感到很兴奋。或许,我的工作就是努力奋斗,永不放弃。这工作就是要让她们提到这件事时会说:"要是她能做到,那么,或许我……"学到的是音乐还是勇气,哪一个更多一些,我难以确定。

6

# TEXT B

# A PRODIGY'S EARLY YEARS

## Background Information

1. **Lang Lang** (Chinese: 郎朗; pinyin: Láng Lǎng) (born June 14, 1982) A virtuoso pianist from Shenyang in Liaoning, China.

   *Early Years*

   Lang Lang was two years old when he saw Tom playing piano in The Cat Concerto, a Tom and Jerry cartoon on TV (Hungarian Rhapsody No. 2 in C-sharp minor composed by Franz Liszt). According to Lang Lang, this first contact with Western music was what motivated him to learn the piano. He began lessons at age three with Professor Zhu Ya-Fen. At the age of five, he won the Shenyang Piano Competition and played his first public recital.

   When he was nine years old, Lang Lang was nearing his audition for Beijing's Central Conservatory of Music, but he had difficulties with his lessons, and was expelled from his piano tutor's studio for lack of talent. His music teacher at his state school noticed Lang Lang's sadness, and decided to comfort him by playing a record of Mozart's Piano Sonata No.10 in C Major, K.330; she asked him to play with the slow movement. This reminded Lang of his love of the instrument. "Playing the K.330 brought me hope again," recalled Lang years later.

   Lang finally entered the Conservatory, studying under Professor Zhao Ping-Guo. In 1993, Lang won the Xing Hai Cup Piano Competition in Beijing, being awarded first prize for outstanding artistic performance at the Fourth International Young Pianists Competition in Germany the next year. In 1995, at 13 years of age, he played the Op. 10 and Op. 25 Chopin Etudes, at Beijing Concert Hall and, in the same year, won first place at the Tchaikovsky International Young Musicians' Competition in Japan, playing Chopin's Piano Concerto No.2 with the Moscow Philharmonic Orchestra in a concert broadcast by NHK Television. At 14 he was a featured soloist at the China National Symphony's inaugural concert, which was broadcast by CCTV and attended by President Jiang Zemin. The following year he began studies with Gary Graffman and Dick Doran at the Curtis Institute in Philadelphia. His most recent published work is the piano work for the score of the movie *The Painted Veil*.

   Lang Lang was recently recognized for his efforts by the United Nations' Children's Fund (UNICEF) who appointed him an international Goodwill Ambassador.

2. **Tchaikovsky** Born April 25 [May 7, New Style], 1840, Votkinsk, Russia, died October 25 [November 6], 1893, St. Petersburg. Tchaikovsky also spelled *Chaikovsky, Chaikovskii,* or *Tschaikowsky* name in full Anglicized as *Peter Ilich Tchaikovsky* the most popular Russian composer of all time. His music has always had great appeal for the general public in virtue of

its tuneful, open-hearted melodies, impressive harmonies, and colorful, picturesque orchestration, all of which evoke a profound emotional response. His oeuvre includes 7 symphonies, 11 operas, 3 ballets, 5 suites, 3 piano concertos, a violin concerto, 11 overtures (strictly speaking, 3 overtures and 8 single movement programmatic orchestral works), 4 cantatas, 20 choral works, 3 string quartets, a string sextet, and more than 100 songs and piano pieces.

## Language Points

1. **prodigy** *n.* a young person who is usually intelligent or skilful for their age
   *Mozart was a musical prodigy.*
   *child/infant prodigy*

2. **instrument** *n.* here refers to musical instrument
   *Is he learning an instrument?*
   *He accompanied her singing on a lutelike instrument.*
   *wind/stringed instruments*

3. **orchestra** *n.* a large group or people who play various musical instruments together, led by a conductor
   *the Berlin Symphony Orchestra / the school orchestra*
   **orchestra section/seats** American English the area of seats in a theatre close to and on the same level as the stage
   **orchestra pit** the space below the stage in a theatre where the musicians sit

4. **keyboard** *n.* the set of black and white keys on a piano or other musical instrument
   *a computer keyboard / a piano keyboard*
   [pl.] an electronic musical instrument similar to a piano that can make sounds like many different instruments

5. **afford** *v.* [no passive] (usually used with can, could, or be able to, especially in negative sentences or questions) to have enough money or time to be able to buy or to do sth
   **can/could afford** [usually negative]
   **afford sth**
   *I couldn't afford the rent on my own.*
   *Dad can't afford any more time off work.*
   **afford to do sth** (*formal*) to provide sth or allow sth to happen
   *We can't afford to wait any longer or we'll miss the plane.*
   **afford (sb) an opportunity/chance**
   *It afforded her the opportunity to improve her tennis skills.*

6. **string** *n.* [C] a tightly stretched piece of wire, nylon or catgut on a musical instrument, that produces a musical note when the instrument is played
   **the strings/the string section** the people in an orchestra or band who play musical instruments that have strings, such as violins

8

*The opening theme is taken up by the strings.*

*He teaches the strings to schoolchildren.*

7. **fortune**   *n. [U]*   chance or luck, especially in the way it affects people's lives

   *I had the good fortune to work with a brilliant head of department.*

   *Sickness or ill fortune could reduce you to a needy situation.*

   *I felt it was useless to struggle against fortune.*

8. **sacrifice**   *n. [C, U]*   the fact of giving up sth important or valuable to you in order to get or do sth that seems more important, sth that you give up in this way

   *The minister stressed the need for economic sacrifice.*

   *The workforce were willing to make sacrifices in order to preserve jobs.*

   *She brought three children up single-handedly, often at great personal sacrifice.*

   *They made sacrifices to ensure a good harvest.*

   *v.*   to willingly stop having sth you want or doing sth you like in order to get sth more important

   **sacrifice sth for sth**

   *A Labor government chose to sacrifice defense for welfare.*

   **sacrifice sth to do sth**

   *He sacrificed a promising career to look after his kids.*

   **sacrifice oneself (for sth)**

   *mothers who sacrifice themselves for their children*

9. **stay behind**   stay in the place where sb/sth is or was

   *They all left the office at five o'clock, but he stayed behind to finish some work.*

   *If you stay behind after class, I will repeat the instructions.*

10. **work at/on sth**   to do sth that involves physical or mental effort, especially as part of a job

    *The greater part of the night he worked at helping to organize the strikers.*

    *He's working at a new invention.*

    *A trainer has been brought in to work on her fitness.*

    **work on doing sth**

    *We need to work on ensuring that the children feel safe and confident.*

11. **start over**   *(esp. AmE)*   to begin again

    *If you make a mistake, just erase it and start over.*

    *She wasn't happy with our work and made us start over.*

12. **funny**   *adj.*   making you laugh, amusing

    *Do you remember any funny stories about work?*

    *If this is your idea of a joke, I don't find it at all funny.*

    *Luckily, when I explained the situation, he saw the funny side (=recognized that it was partly funny).*

    *His laughter stopped her mid-sentence. "What's so funny?" she demanded.*

13. **accent**   *n. [C, U]*   the way of producing the words of a language that shows which country or area a person comes from

    *He noticed that I spoke Polish with an accent.*

English/American/Indian etc. accent
a broad/strong/slight/faint etc. accent

14. **look after**   to take of someone by helping them, giving them what they need, or keeping them safe

    Who's going to look after the children while you're away?

    I'm looking after his affairs while he is in hospital.

    Don't worry about me—I can look after myself.

    He's good at looking after his own interests.

15. **miserable**   *adj.*   very unhappy or uncomfortable

    I've been so miserable since Patrick left me.

    I spent the weekend feeling miserable.

    Janice looks really miserable.

    Why do you make yourself miserable by taking on too much work?

16. **devastate**   *v.*   to completely destroy a place or an area

    Rob was devastated by the news of her death.

    The city centre was devastated by the bomb.

17. **push**   *v.*   to persuade or encourage sb to do sth that they may not want to do

    Encourage your kids to try new things, but try not to push them too hard.

    athletes who push their bodies to the limit

    **push oneself**

    He's been pushing himself too hard, working 12-hour days.

    **push sb into (doing) sth**

    My husband pushed me into leaving the job.

    **push sb to do sth**

    The teachers pushed the students to achieve.

18. **turn around**   to start being successful after it has been unsuccessful for a time

    The company turned around from losses of 1.4 million last year to profits of 26,800.

    At Rockwell International he had turned around a badly performing division.

    After I met him, my whole life turned around.

# Answer Keys

## I. Getting the Message

### Section A

1. NG   2. Y   3. N   4. Y   5. N   6. Y

### Section B

1. his parents             2. stayed behind in Shenyang
3. not enough money        4. take a bus

5. give it up      6. play some holiday songs

## II. Recognizing Main Ideas

1. pianist      2. young      3. sacrificed      4. concertmaster      5. moved
6. devastated      7. give up      8. talent      9. realize      10. after all

## 参考译文

### 天才早年

我是一个生长在中国沈阳的男孩,每天练习钢琴6个小时。我喜欢钢琴这种乐器。母亲教我识谱,父亲教我如何把握琴键。父亲是当地一个民间管弦乐队的首席小提琴手。开始的时候,我在国产键盘乐器上练习,这种乐器价格低廉,但就我们的财力而言却是最好的键盘乐器。后来,父母给我买了一台瑞典钢琴,我却在练习柴可夫斯基的乐曲时弄坏了一半的琴弦。这时,父母觉得这台钢琴以及我的家乡已经不能满足我的需求了,要成为一名了不起的钢琴家,就要去我们的文化之都——北京。

我的父亲会拉二胡,这是一种两根弦的乐器。他告诉我生活会很艰辛。他说我需要机会,如果不努力,就不会有机会。

为了和我一同迁居北京,父亲做出了很大的牺牲。他辞去了首席小提琴手的工作,他很喜欢这份工作,母亲留在了沈阳,继续上班来供养我们。父母都警告过我:"做钢琴家很难,母亲不在身边,你能生活吗?"我说:"我要和母亲在一起。"可我知道我必须去北京。在美国,人们经常搬来搬去,在中国却行不通,至少在那些日子里不行。

突然间,父亲和我就成了新移民——客居他乡的外乡人。对我们周围的人来说,我们操着滑稽的北方口音,唯一能租得起的公寓是在一幢没有供暖的大楼里,5个家庭共用一个卫生间。父亲为我做饭、打扫房间、照顾我,基本上就成了一个家庭主妇。

我们住的地方离学校很远,坐公交车又太贵,父亲就每天"驾"着自行车接送我,一趟就是一个半小时的路程,加上我身体沉重,但即便是冬天父亲也是日日如此。夜里最冷的时候,我练琴练累时,父亲躺在床上给我暖被窝。

我感到很痛苦,并不是因为贫穷和压力,是因为北京的新老师并不喜欢我,她经常对我说:"你没有天赋,永远成不了钢琴家。"终于有一天,她把我"扫地出门"。

那时我刚刚9岁,我彻底垮了,再也不想当钢琴家了。接下来的两个星期里,我连钢琴都没有碰过。父亲很明智,并没有劝说,他只是在等待。

那一天终于来临了。学校的老师要我弹奏几首节日歌曲,我不想弹。可当我的手指放在钢琴琴键上时,我意识到我能向别人证明我有天赋。

那天,我说出了父亲一直想听到的话——我想和一位新老师学琴。从那时起,一切都峰回路转、柳暗花明了。

英语阅读的瓶颈——词汇多义性 What Does It Really Mean?

**阅读技巧例证补充**

以下都是学生熟悉的词汇,但这些词汇在以下三个专业中却具有截然不同的意义,这里举例补充一些。鼓励学生以自己所学专业为基础,积累记忆相关词汇。

| Music | flag(音符的)符尾 | head(音符的)符头 | major 大调 | time 拍子 |
|---|---|---|---|---|
| | strings 弦乐器 | neck 琴颈 | bow 琴弓 | bridge 琴马 |
| | sharp 升号 | flat 降号 | | |
| Sports | head 头球 | shot 铅球 | long jump 跳远 | judge 裁判 | high bar 单杠 |
| | floor exercise 体操 | goal 球门 | base 垒 | net 球网 | try 带球触地 |
| Fine Arts | model 模特 | brush 画笔 | studio 画室 | work 作品 | watercolor 水彩 |
| | portrait 画像 | artist 画家 | fine arts 美术 | wash 水墨画 | study 习作 |

I. Direction: You are asked to read the following three groups of sentences and write down the meaning of the italic words in Chinese in the blanks.(Two blanks for each word. The first blank is for the meaning you learnt before, another for the meaning in the context given here. Use the dictionary if necessary. )

| band | 带、绳 | 乐队 | choirs | 群、组、队 | 合唱团 |
| record | 记录 | (体育)记录 | event | 事件 | 赛事 |
| brush | 刷子 | 画笔 | work | 工作 | 作品 |

II. Direction: Examine what the students have got from the internet resource given in the classroom.

# Unit Two

# Championship

## Script for Lead-in Listening

Listen to the following conversation and fill in the blanks with the correct words or phrases. You may choose the words or phrases from the list given.

**Pauline:** Look, the match is going to start.
**Bill:** Yes. I guess it'll be an exciting match between two strong teams.
**Pauline:** Well, team A's won the toss.
**Bill:** So team B's retreating to their own half of the field.
**Pauline:** Look! No.8 on team A is going to pass. He's my favorite player. A long pass..., and No. 6 has got it.
**Bill:** No. 6 is taking the ball forward quickly. He seems to be a playmaker.
**Pauline:** You've got it. What's the matter? The referee is whistling for a foul.
**Bill:** The forward fouled in the penalty area. It's going to be a corner kick ...
**Pauline:** Team B's defense is well organized today... What a beautiful center!
**Bill:** I like this game. The competition is so fierce.
**Pauline:** Oh, my! No 7 has just missed an open goal.
**Bill:** Don't get nervous. We still have a chance in the first half. Look, No.6 has just given a long shot ...

## WORDS AND EXPRESSIONS IN LEAD-IN LISTENING

**fierce** *adj.* showing strong feelings or a lot of activity, often in a way that is violent
  *Competition from abroad became fierce in the 1990s.*
**pass** *v.* (in football, hockey, etc.) to kick, hit or throw the ball to a player of your own side
  *Why do they keep passing back to the goalie?*
**playmaker** *n.* a player who leads the offense for a team
**referee** *n.* an official who controls the game in some sports, such as football, basketball and boxing
  *He was sent off for arguing with the referee.*
**foul** *n.* an action that is against the rules of the game
  *It was a clear foul by Ford on the goalkeeper.*
**penalty area** (British also **penalty box**) (in football) the area in front of the goal. If the defending team breaks the rules within this area, the other team is given a penalty

**corner kick** (also **corner**) (in football) a free kick that you take from the corner of your opponent's end of the field

**defense** *n.* the players who must prevent the other team from scoring; the position of these players on the sports

*Welford cut through the defense to score the winning goal.*

**center** *n.* passing the ball to the middle

**open goal** one that had nobody defending it

**long shot** kicking the ball from a distance

# TEXT A

## A DREAM COMES TRUE

### Background Information

1. **Ricardo Izecson dos Santos Leite** (better known as **Kaká**) A Brazilian midfielder who plays for Italian Serie A club A.C. Milan and the Brazilian national team. He was instrumental in Milan's 2006-2007 Champions League triumph, which earned him the Ballond'Or and FIFA World Player of the Year awards in 2007.

*Early life*

Kaká was born to Simone Cristina dos Santos Leite and Bosco Izecson Pereira Leite. He has a younger brother, Rodrigo (known as Digão), who has followed in his footsteps by playing football for Milan.

At the age of 18, Kaká suffered a career-threatening and possibly paralysis-inducing spinal fracture as a result of a swimming pool accident, but remarkably made a full recovery. He attributes his recovery to God and has since tithed his income to his church.

*Club career*

Kaká began his club career with São Paulo at the age of eight. He signed a contract at 15 and led the SPFC youth squad to *Copa de Juvenil* glory. Kaká made his senior side debut in January 2001 and scored 12 goals in 27 appearances, in addition to leading São Paulo to its first and only Torneio Rio-São Paulo championship. He scored 10 in 22 matches the following season, and by this time his performance was soon attracting attention from European clubs.

AC Milan, fresh from winning the 2003 Champions League, brought him aboard in 2003 for $8.5 million, a fee described in hindsight as "peanuts" by club owner Silvio Berlusconi. Within a month, he cracked the starting lineup, and has remained there since. His Serie A debut was in a 2-0 Milan win at A.C. Ancona. He scored 10 goals in 30 appearances that season, as Milan won the Scudetto and the European Super Cup.

The 2005-2006 season saw Kaká score his first hat-tricks in domestic and European competition. On April 9, 2006, he scored his first Rossoneri hat-trick against Chievo Verona. All three goals were scored in the second half. Seven months later, he scored his first Champions League hat-trick in a 4-1 group stage win over RSC Anderlecht. The football world was beginning to take notice of a superstar in the making. Following Rui Costa's departure to Benfica at the end of the season, and despite the insistence of many Milan fans, Kaká turned down the chance to switch from his number 22 to the now-vacant number 10, a number typically associated with world-class playmakers. (The number was eventually claimed by teammate Clarence Seedorf.)

*Nickname*

His nickname is pronounced as it is spelled, with stress on the second syllable. It is a common term of endearment of "Ricardo" in Brazil. In Kaká's case, however, it was born from younger brother Rodrigo, who is now known as Digao, calling him "Caca" due to his inability to pronounce "Ricardo" when they were young; it eventually evolved into Kaká. He is occasionally called "Ricky Kaká" by the European media.

2. **The Ballon d'Or award** (French for Golden Ball) An association football award, created in 1956 by the French football magazine *France Football*. Until 2007 it was usually known in English as the *European Footballer of the Year* award. Ballon d'Or is widely regarded as the most prestigious individual award in football.

The award is given annually to the player considered to have performed the best over the previous year. Prior to 2007, the player had to be a member of a club based within UEFA's jurisdiction, in order to qualify for selection. Until 1995, a player also had to be of European nationality to be eligible. From 1995 to 2006 any player from a European club was eligible, regardless of his nationality. In October 2007 *France Football* announced that their new list of nominees includes players from around the globe, regardless of the league they play in.

Voting for the award is undertaken by a group of football journalists. Each voter chooses five players from the list of 50 nominees established by *France Football*, and awards them one, two, three, four and five points. The winner is determined by the total number of points. Players who finish second and third in the voting are awarded silver and bronze medals.

3. **Lionel Messi** (born 24 June 1987 in Rosario) An Argentine international footballer who currently plays for FC Barcelona in the Primera División, and for the Argentine national team. He has drawn comparisons to Diego Maradona, and indeed Maradona himself named Messi his "successor".

4. **Christino Ronaldo Cristiano Ronaldo dos Santos Aveiro** (born 5 February 1985 in Funchal, Madeira, better known as **Cristiano Ronaldo**) A Portuguese professional footballer. He plays both for the English Premier League club Manchester United and the Portuguese national team. With Manchester United, Ronaldo plays primarily as a right winger. He has also been used both in a central attacking role and as a second striker. A winner of the 2007 English PFA Player and Young Player of the Year awards and third in the 2007 World Player of the Year award, Ronaldo is widely regarded as one of the most talented footballers of his generation

**5. FIFA** The Federation Internationale de Football Association (**International Federation of Association Football**, commonly known by its acronym, **FIFA**) The international governing body of association football. Its headquarters is in Zürich, Switzerland, and its current president is Joseph Blatter. FIFA is responsible for the organization and governance of football's major international tournaments, most notably the FIFA World Cup, held since 1930.

FIFA has 208 member associations, which is 16 more than the United Nations and 3 more than the International Olympic Committee.

## Language Points

1. **come true** (of a hope, wish, etc.) to become reality

   *The prediction seems to have come true.*

   *He wondered whether the prophecy would come true.*

2. **finalist** *n.* a person who takes part in the final, of a game or a competition

   *She and a panel of judges will choose 10 finalists, and the winner.*

   *The 12 finalists were chosen from more than 250 entries from across the nation.*

   *Three to five finalists will be announced on April 19.*

3. **award** *n. [C]* a prize such as money, etc. for sth that sb has done

   **award for**

   *the Presidential Award for Excellence in Science and Mathematics Teaching*

   **win/receive an award**

   *Rosie was in London to receive her award as Mum of the Year.*

   *The hotel's award-winning restaurant specializes in traditional food.*

4. **aspire** *v.* to have a strong desire to achieve or to become sth

   *How he must have aspired to rise up forcefully.*

   *Laura had always aspired to the very best within a certain budget.*

   *At that time, all serious artists aspired to go to Rome.*

5. **vote** *v.* to show formally by making a paper or raising your hand which person you want to win an election, or which plan or idea you support

   *In 1918 British women got the right to vote.*

   **vote for/against/in favour of**

   *I voted for the Labor candidate in the last election.*

   *53% of Danes voted in favor of the Maastricht treaty.*

   **vote on**

   *The people of Ulster had finally been given a chance to vote on the issue.*

   **vote to do sth**

   *Congress voted to increase foreign aid by 10%.*

   *Shareholders voted to reject the offer.*

6. **accolade** *n.* praise or an award for an achievement that people admire

   *Already, the program has won accolades for bringing investment to poor neighborhoods*

of Knoxville.

7. **acclaim**   n. [U]   praise and approval for sb/sth, especially an artistic achievement
   *The young singer is enjoying massive critical acclaim (=praised by people who are paid to give their opinion on art, music etc.).*

8. **critic**   n.   a person who expresses opinions about the good and bad qualities of books, music, etc.
   *Daley accused critics of the city's Police Department of lying.*
   *Film critic Roger Ebert has a new partner for his movie-review television program.*
   *Critics of the scheme have said that it will not solve the problem of teenage crime.*

9. **incredible**   adj.   impossible or very difficult to believe
   *It is incredible that the police still haven't caught him.*
   *She's an incredible dancer.*
   *The divorce rate in the US is pretty incredible.*

10. **highlight**   n.   the best, most interesting or most exciting part of sth
    *Highlights of the ball game will be shown later.*
    *Before the game, fans were shown highlights of the season on a large video screen.*
    *That weekend in Venice was definitely the highlight of our trip.*

11. **go for sth**   to choose sth
    *I think I'll go for the fruit Salad.*

12. **milestone**   n.   a very important stage or event in the development of sth
    *For most people, the birth of their first child is a milestone in their lives.*
    *Graduation and marriage are important milestones in people's lives.*
    *His decision to accept the university's offer was an important milestone in his career.*

13. **trophy**   n.   an object such as a silver-cup that is given as a prize for winning a competition
    *He kept the antlers as a trophy.*
    *The winner went to receive her trophy.*

14. **be determined to do sth**   if you are determined to do sth, you have made a firm decision to do it and you will not let anyone prevent you
    *Both sides in the dispute seemed determined not to compromise.*
    *I was determined to be a professional dancer, and practiced for hours every day.*
    *She was determined to win.*

15. **identify**   v.   to recognize sb/sth and be able to say who or what they are
    *After years of research, scientists have identified the virus that is responsible for the disease.*
    *Can you identify the man who robbed you?*
    **identify sb/sth as sb/sth**
    *Eye witnesses identified the gunman as an army sergeant.*
    *The aircraft were identified as American.*

16. **thereabouts**   adv.   (usually used after *or*) near the place mentioned; used to say that a particular number, quantity, time, etc. is not exact
    *A series of connected events occurred in the tenth century or thereabouts.*

*All the land thereabouts was once in the possession of the powerful Vachel family.*
*It looked like a 1950 model, thereabouts.*

17. **tournament**  *n.*  a sports competition, involving a number of teams or players who take part in different games and most leave the competition if they lose. The competition continues until there is only the winner

*Telford won the local five-a-side football tournament.*
*There's a volleyball tournament at Sunset Park which begins today.*

18. **sort out**  to deal with sb who is causing trouble, etc. especially by punishing or attacking them; to organize sth in a satisfactory way

*It took quite a while to sort out our luggage.*
*It takes some time to sort out my thoughts before I can start writing.*

19. **cope with**  to deal successfully with sth difficult.

*She feared she wouldnt be able to cope with two new babies.*
*Local authorities have to cope with the problems of homelessness.*

20. **take sth on**  to decide to do sth; to agree to be responsible for sb/sth

*Don't take on too much work—the extra cash isn't worth it.*

# Answer Keys

## I. Getting the Message
1. C    2. B    3. D    4. A    5. B

## II. Developing Your Vocabulary

### Section A
1. final    2. award    3. vote    4. incredible    5. highlights    6. identification

### Section B
1. came through    2. sort out    3. out of    4. go for    5. take on    6. cope with

## III. Recognizing Main Ideas
1. finalist    2. interview    3. wonderful    4. critics
5. highly    6. games    7. confidence    8. fight

## IV. Trying the Translation

### Section A
1. 感觉棒极了。跻身世界前三甲足球队员之列是梦想成真。
2. 你如何评价与你一起进入决赛的利昂内尔·梅西和克里斯蒂亚诺·罗纳尔多？
3. 我认为是赢得欧洲联赛冠军杯,那是我生命中的一个里程碑。
4. 我相信我们会很快找出原因,米兰会重整旗鼓,像往常一样奋力拼搏。

5. 每个成就的取得都使我意识到,我为我所效力的俱乐部和我的国家所承担的责任越来越多。

## Section B

1. Every one wants to reach the top in his /her career.
2. It's important to win acclaim from other players.
3. He has an incredible talent and wonderful future in front of him in playing football.
4. What's your dream for 2008 Olympics?
5. We are going to come through a difficult spell, and we have to work harder.

## V. Organizing Your Ideas

b   e   c   d   f   a

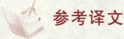
参考译文

### 梦想成真

**FIFA.COM：** 进入本年度世界足球先生决赛,你感觉如何?

**卡卡：** 感觉棒极了。跻身世界前三甲足球队员之列是梦想成真,是每一位足球运动员都渴望达到的高度,这让我尤其开心。

**FIFA.COM：** 金球奖是由足球评论家评出的,而世界足球先生是由国家队队长和教练们决定的,感觉有什么不一样吗?

**卡卡：** 这两个奖是非常不同的。赢得评论家与媒体的称赞很重要,得到教练与球员的肯定同样重要。今年我很幸运,同时获得了这两方面的支持。

**FIFA.COM：** 你如何评价与你一起进入决赛的利昂内尔·梅西和克里斯蒂亚诺·罗纳尔多?

**卡卡：** 他们两位都是伟大的足球运动员,天赋惊人,前程不可限量。他们也都很年轻。事实上,我 25 岁了,是三个人中年龄最大的。这说明才华横溢的新一代正崭露头角。

**FIFA.COM：** 今年对你来说精彩纷呈。你获得的众多成就中,最精彩的又是哪一项呢?

**卡卡：** 我认为应该是赢得欧洲联赛冠军杯,那是我生命中的一个里程碑,一个真正的高度。欧洲联赛冠军杯是最重要的俱乐部锦标赛。

**FIFA.COM：** 你是全世界最好的足球运动员之一,你鼓舞了许多人,又是什么激励着你前进呢?

**卡卡：** 小时候,雷始终是激励我的那个人,他曾先后效力于圣保罗队与巴黎圣日尔曼队。在我成长的那些年,他是获得许多冠军称号的一流球队圣保罗队的明星球员。那时候我想努力超越他。

**FIFA.COM：** 2008 年你的梦想是什么?

**卡卡：** 我的目标是继续赢得比赛。欧洲联赛冠军杯是最重大的奖项,但意大利足球甲级联赛也很重要。AC 米兰永远心向胜利,这个赛季我们一定能赢得双份。

**FIFA.COM:** AC米兰在国际比赛中表现出色,但在意甲联赛中却困难重重。原因在哪呢?

**卡卡:** 我们正处在国内联赛夺冠的困难时期,但仍未找出问题所在。在国际联赛中米兰成绩一向不错,我们正在努力改变国内联赛的局面。我相信我们会很快找出原因,米兰会重整旗鼓,像往常一样奋力拼搏。

**FIFA.COM:** 在巴西队中,你正逐渐成为一名领袖。你是如何应对这种情况的?

**卡卡:** 每个成就的取得都使我意识到,我为我所效力的俱乐部和我的国家所承担的责任越来越多。但我已经学会处理这些事情,这对我来说完全不成问题。

# TEXT B

## REAL CHAMPIONS

### Background Information

**1. Lleyton Hewitt** (born 24 February 1981)　A former World No. 1 tennis player from Australia. In 2001, he became the youngest male ever to be ranked number one. His career best achievements are winning the 2001 US Open and 2002 Wimbledon men's singles titles. In 2005, *Tennis* Magazine put Hewitt in 34th place on its list of the 40 greatest tennis players since 1965. Hewitt is currently ranked 20 in the world.

Hewitt is known for his competitiveness and wins most of his matches with relentless aggression, fitness, consistent shots, and highly skilled footwork. Hewitt spent much time in the late stages of 2004 working with his former coach and good friend, Roger Rasheed, on bulking up his physique. His hard work paid off after he made it to the final of the 2005 Australian Open, before losing to Marat Safin in 4 sets (1-6 6-3 6-4 6-4).

**2. Wimbledon**　The Championships, Wimbledon, commonly referred to as Wimbledon, is the oldest major championship in tennis.

Held annually between late June and the beginning of July for two weeks (usually ending, at the latest, on the second Sunday of July) at the All England Lawn Tennis and Croquet Club in London, England, the tournament is the third Grand Slam event played each year, preceded by the Australian Open and the French Open, and followed by the US Open. The tournament duration is subject to extensions for rain.

Separate tournaments are simultaneously held, all at the same venue, for Gentlemen's Singles, Ladies' Singles, Gentlemen's Doubles, Ladies' Doubles and Mixed Doubles. Youth tournaments—Boys' Singles, Girls' Singles, Boys' Doubles and Girls' Doubles—are also held. Additionally, special invitational tournaments are held: the 35 and over Gentlemen's Doubles, 45 and over Gentlemen's Doubles, 35 and over Ladies' Doubles and Wheelchair Doubles.

## Language Points

1. **compete with/against**  *v.*  to try to be more successful or better than sb else who is trying to do the same as you

    They found themselves competing with foreign companies for a share of the market.
    We can't compete with them on price.

2. **potentially**  *adv.*  sth that is potentially dangerous, useful etc. is not dangerous etc. now, but may become so in the future

    a potentially fatal disease
    Sculpture workshops are potentially dangerous work sites.

3. **feat**  *n.*  an action or piece of work that needs skill, strength or courage

    He led his team to victory for the tenth time, a feat no captain had achieved before.
    The tunnel is a brilliant feat of enginnering.

4. **barrier**  *n.*  a problem, rule or situation that prevents sb from doing sth, or that makes sth impossible

    The driver slowed down as he approached the police barrier.
    The police put up barriers to hold back the crowds.
    We want to break down barriers between doctors and patients.

5. **come down to sth**  to be able to be explained by a single important point

    Our choices come down to going or staying.

6. **take pride in**  to do sth very carefully and well in a way that gives you a lot of satisfaction

    He takes great pride in his children's achievements.
    Your should take more pride in your work.
    She took great pride in her appearance.

7. **distract**  *v.*  to take sb's attention away from what they are trying to do

    Don't distract me while I'm driving!
    Don't distract your father while he's driving.
    I was distracted by the sound of a car alarm in the street.

8. **peer**  *n.* [usually pl.]  a person who is the same age or who has the same social status as you

    At about three years old, children begin to take an interest in their peers.
    Everyone wants to be successful in the eyes of their peers.
    The jury system gives you the basic right to be judged by your peers.

9. **substitute**  *n.*  a person or thing that you use or have instead of the one you normally use or have

    If Marsh has not fully recovered, his likely substitute will be Robinson.
    Ten minutes into the second half Davies was brought on as substitute for Ward.
    The coach has to find a substitute for Tim.

10. **maxim**　*n.*　a well-known phrase that expresses sth that is usually true or that people think is a rule for sensible behavior

   That's always been one of Father's maxims.
   I share the same maxim with my best friend.

11. **routinely**　*adv.*　if sth is routinely done, it is done as a normal part of a process or job

   Visitors are routinely checked as they enter the building.
   The cars are routinely tested for safety and reliability before leaving the factory.

12. **deter**　*v.*　to make sb decide not to do sth or continue doing sth especially by making them understand the difficulties and unpleasant results of their actions

   It is not clear whether the death penalty deters crime.
   The new alarm system should deter car thieves.

13. **build up**　to become greater, more powerful or larger in number

   Exercises build up muscles.
   You must build up your strength again.
   Your brother has the nicest manners, but he needs building up.

14. **look back on**　to think about sth that happened in the past

   When I look back on those days I realize I was desperately unhappy.
   Looking back on it, I still can't figure out what went wrong.

15. **dig deep and put in the hard yard**　to practice a lot and to be patient

16. **pay off**　to be successful and bring good results

   Did your plan pay off?
   It was a risk but it paid off.

17. **put one's noses to the grindstone**　(*informal*) to work hard for a long period of time without stooping

   Now is the time for the golfer from Welwyn Garden City to put his nose to the grindstone once more.

18. **exceptional**　*adj.*　unusually good

   A few of the top executives are women, but this is still exceptional.
   Exit visas are only given in exceptional circumstances.
   Graham Greene had exceptional talents as a story-teller.

19. **ethic**　*n.*　moral principles that control or influence a person's behavior

   Televised news is based on a code of ethics .
   He began to questionhis ethics of his position.

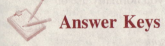

# Answer Keys

## I. Getting the Message

### Section A

1. Y　　2. N　　3. N　　4. Y　　5. N　　6. NG

## Section B

1. share the same qualities
2. to break his own best reord
3. drive them forward
4. what hard work means to them
5. gained confidence again
6. the top people in other fields

## II. Recognizing Main Ideas

1. challenging  2. qualities  3. determination  4. break  5. sporting career
6. plays  7. failed  8. training  9. gold medals  10. top people

## 参考译文

### 冠军品质

运动员与别人竞技是理所当然的事情,但对冠军而言,最大的竞争却是来自于自己。我们不妨了解一下温布尔登网球公开赛冠军,世界网球排名第一雷登·休伊特的想法。尽管他自己被视为澳大利亚最伟大的运动天才之一,甚至可能成为世界上有史以来最好的球员之一,他还是相信能做得更好。今年早些时候,他告诉媒体:"我觉得过去几年我的表现不尽人意,实际上,即使名列榜首,我也做得不够好。"

另外一位运动员是奥运会和世界1500米游泳冠军格兰特·哈克特,他很喜欢打破自己的纪录。在去年世界游泳锦标赛上他创造了一项新的世界纪录:14:34.56,之后在8月份的泛太平洋运动会上,他游出了这项赛事历史上第二个最快速度纪录:14:41.65。现在,哈克特的目标是突破14分这个屏障。格登认为,这种决心源自对自己以及自己所从事的事业的自豪感。他说:"冠军不是以别人的表现来评判自己,其判断的标准完全是自己的表现。"

这种规律也适用于生活中的其他领域。大学学业有成和从政舞台上春风得意的人不会受到其他人成就的影响,而是专注于自己的目标。

真正的冠军知道没有什么可以替代有益的、传统意义上的艰苦努力。这也是一位深受人们喜爱的澳大利亚网球选手的座右铭。由于缺乏经验,他经常输给那些强手。有人建议他不必再费时费力去申请参加澳大利亚体育学院的网球培训了。但他不是一个就此止步的人,他不断拼搏,通过艰苦的努力建立了自己的实力和名望。今天,帕特里克·拉夫特可以回顾所取得的两场大满贯胜利了。他已经名列世界头号选手,今年又被选为澳大利亚年度人物。

这种不怕吃苦、待机而动的能力也是激励游泳选手麦克尔·克里姆的一种品质。他参加了1996年亚特兰大奥运会200米自由泳项目,当时排名世界第一,却出人意料地没能进入决赛。失望之余,他回到家乡,他知道要想重新夺冠,就必须在泳池中接受残酷的训练。两年之后,艰苦努力终于得到了回报:他赢得了4枚英联邦运动会金牌,在佩斯举行的世界锦标赛上获得7枚金牌。

帕特里克·拉夫特和麦克尔·克里姆成为教科书中的典范人物,展示了冠军是如何通过不懈努力而获得成功的。格登说:"即使具有非凡的天赋,没有艰苦努力也是不能成功的。同样,这句话也适用于那些时装设计师、企业家、作曲家和外科医生。任何领域的顶尖人物都清楚:没有艰苦努力,就没有成功。

# Reading in Focus

英语长、难句的阅读 Understand Long Sentences (1)

## EXERCISES

I. Direction: Read the following sentences selected from the Text A and B carefully. Analyze the underlined parts which are complicated, tell how complicated they are, Then write down theirgrammatical functions they have in the brackets.

1. 主语(带有定语从句)　　2. 介词宾语(带有定语从句)　　3. 表语(带有定语从句)
4. 宾语(带有定语从句)　　5. 宾语(从句)　　　　　　　　6. 介词宾语(从句)
7. 主语(带有定语从句)　　8. 表语(带有定语从句)

II. Direction: Translate the following groups of sentences into English and compare to see how a long or complicated sentence is formed.

1. Tom is a college student.
   - Tom who comes from America is a college student.
     - Tome who comes from America is a college student who graduated from Harvard university.

2. Our president visited an American city.
   - Our president who had retired recently visited an American city.
     - Our president who had retired recently visited an American city which has a large population.

3. Children are watching a cartoon.
   - Children who finished drawing are watching a cartoon.
     - Children who finished drawing are watching a cartoon which the teacher rented.

4. There are many pianos in the classroom.
   - There are many pianos which the college bought this term in the classroom.
     - There are many pianos which the college bought this term in the classroom which was newly decorated.

# Unit Three

# Life in Art

 ## Script for Lead-in Listening

Listen to the following conversation and fill in the blanks with the correct words or phrases. You may choose the words or phrases from the list given.

Max: What kind of fine art do you like?
Laura: Well, I like different kinds.
Max: Any in particular?
Laura: Er, I especially like Chinese folk art.
Max: Wow, that's marvelous!
Laura: I'm crazy about Chinese paper-cuts. It's one of the folk arts and traditional decorative arts which China has popularized the most.
Max: What are the subjects of paper-cuts?
Laura: In the past, cutouts came in a wide variety of subjects such as flowers, dragons, gods and fierce animals.
Max: Do they have special meaning?
Laura: All were symbols of good fortune.
Max: It's said that paper-cuts were usually on red paper.
Laura: Yeah. The subject also depended greatly on the occasion: the shapes of gods for New Years, pine trees and cranes for birthdays (symbols of long life), and folklore of the moon for harvest festivals.
Max: Really? That sounds great!

## WORDS AND EXPRESSIONS IN LEAD-IN LISTENING

**fine arts** (also **fine art**) art or forms of art that appeal to the sense of beauty, e.g. painting, sculpture, etc. 美术或美术的各种形式(如绘画,雕刻等)
   *She's doing a course in fine art.*
**marvelous** *adj.* astonishing; wonderful 不可思议的,惊奇的,奇妙的
   *It's marvelous how he's managed to climb that far.*
**decorative** *adj.* that makes sth look more beautiful 装饰的,作装饰用的
   *Decorative work crafted in leather.*
**depend upon/on** be decided by sth; follow from sth 视某事物而定,取决于某事物

*Our success depend on your assistance*

**crane** *n. [C]* large bird with long legs, neck and beak 鹤

*A crane is a bird.*

**folklore** *n. [U]* (study of the) traditions, stories, customs, etc of a community 民间传统，民间故事，民俗

*The mother often tells her children fairy tales and story from folklore.*

# CLAY FIGURINES

## Background Information

**1. Clay Figurine Zhang**   The painted Clay Figurine Zhang in Tianjin is a prestigious Chinese traditional folk art. It originated by Zhang Mingshan during Daoguang Years in the Qing Dynasty, and passed down for four generations till today. Clay Figurine Zhang has a 180-year history. The artist adopted realistic methods to portray the shape of the figure. Zhang inherited the legacy of traditional Chinese clay figurine making skills and also incorporated skills from other art forms such as painting, opera singing and Chinese folk wood engravings. Clay Figurine Zhang has become an absolute vivid original plastic art style. It was highly praised by many maestros, like Guo Moruo, Zhao puchu, Wu Zuoren and Xu Beihong.

The Clay Figurine Zhang is a kind of indoor decorative sculpture and is used widely. Each one is about 40cm in height. Its small size makes it a terrific bookshelf ornament. It plays an important role in beautifying circumstances.

It takes about 30 days to finish a piece of complete clay figurine. Packed with traditional Chinese wrapper, therefore, the splendid artwork of Clay Figurine Zhang is more attractive.

**2. Huishan Clay Figurines**   Made in Wuxi in Jiangsu Province, one of the famous folk arts in China for its succinct design, bright color and vivid image.

It is said that Huishan clay figurines have a history of over 1,000 years, originating in the Northern and Southern Dynasties Period (386—581). It reached the peak during the Ming Dynasty (1368-1644). By the end of the Qing Dynasty (1644—1911), a lot of specialized workshops emerged, and the figures usually molded on the opera actors and actresses for Kunqu (Kun opera) were very popular at that time. The little clay figures are not only very cute and colorful, but also full of cultural connotations in them.

In the 1930s, the craft of clay figures absorbed techniques of gesso engraving, and developed a special Huishan school of clay figures. Since the founding of new China, the craft has made great progress with support of the government. In the 1950s, a number of specialized factories and institutions were established one after another.

The black and sticky local soil has been used to make clay figurines, and the process has three steps. There are mainly two types of the figurines, one molded and the other made by hand. The molded clay figures are relatively coarse and good as toys for kids. The hand-made figures are more delicate, creative and vivid, having a variety of characters that are largely based on traditional Chinese operas and the rich Chinese culture.

Huishan clay figures have been exported to more than 60 countries and regions and invited to take part in many cultural exchange activities, marking a great contribution to Sino-foreign cultural exchanges.

## Language Points

1. **favor**  *n. [U]*  liking; goodwill; approval
   He has never looked on any of my ideas with favor.
   Senior ministers spoke in favor of the proposal.
   I talked to Susie about it, and she' all in favor (= completely approves) of going.

2. **delicate**  *adj.*  very carefully made or formed; fine; exquisite
   the delicate beauty of a snowflake
   There's something I have to speak to you about—it's a delicate matter.
   Her wrists and ankles were slim and delicate.

3. **initiate**  *v.*  to put (a scheme, etc.) into operation; cause (sth) to begin
   I have a vivid memory of my first day at school.
   They have decided to initiate legal proceedings against the newspaper.
   Intellectuals have initiated a debate on terrorism.

4. **vivid**  *adj.*  producing strong clear pictures in the mind
   His fiancée is a vivid young dancer.
   I've got vivid memories of that summer.
   He had a vivid picture of her in his mind.

5. **nickname**  *n. [C]*  familiar or humorous name given to a person instead of or as well as his real name, often a short form of the real name, or a reference to the person's character, etc.
   As he was always cheerful he had the nickname "Smiler".
   We had nicknames for all the teachers.
   Stephen earned himself the nickname Hawkeye.

6. **distinguish**  *v.*  to recognize the difference between (people or things)
   Speech distinguishes the man from the animals.
   Elephants are distinguished by their long noses/ trunks.
   His attorney argued that Cope could not distinguish between right and wrong.

7. **depict**  *v.*  to show (sb/sth) as a picture; portray
   a book depicting life in pre-revolutionary Russia
   The god is depicted as a bird with a human head.

The drawing depicts her sitting on a sofa.

8. **bulge** *v.* to form a bulge; swell outwards

   His pockets were bulging with candy.

   He fell heavily to the floor, his eyes bulging wide with fear.

   I can't eat any more. My stomach's bulging.

9. **stand out** be easily seen; be noticeable

   She always stood out in a crowd.

   The outlines of rooftops and chimneys stood out against the pale sky.

   I am sure illnesses stand out in all childhood memories.

10. **murderous** *adj.* intending or likely to murder

    murderous drug dealers

    a group of murderous thugs

11. **forsake** *v.* to give (sth) up; to renounce

    forsake one's family and friends

    She will never forsake her vegetarian principles.

    They felt that their leader had forsaken them in their hour of need.

12. **promote** *v.* to help the progress of (sth); encourage or support new efforts to promote the cause of world peace

    Fertilizer promotes leaf growth.

    The organization works to promote friendship between nations.

13. **slack** *adj.* not tight or tense; loose

    She was shocked at the slack discipline in the school.

    Don't get slack at your work.

    Business remained slack throughout the day.

14. **facial** *adj.* of or for the face

    The cream dissolves facial hair.

    Victor's facial expression didn't change.

15. **apply sth ( to sth )** make practical use of sth

    These ideas are often difficult to apply in practice.

    Apply as much force as is necessary.

16. **unique** *adj.* being the only one of its type

    Each person's voice is unique.

    That building is unique because all the others like it were destroyed.

    Traditional American beer is unique.

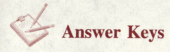
# Answer Keys

## I. Getting the Message
1. C    2. D    3. D    4. B    5. C

## II. Developing Your Vocabulary
### Section A
1. forsake    2. unique    3. murderous    4. representative    5. promote    6. delicate

### Section B
1. applied to    2. at any time    3. is adept at
4. all walks of life    5. make a living    6. stood out

## III. Recognizing Main Ideas
1. figurines    2. traditional    3. created    4. unique
5. at home and abroad    6. as well as    7. different    8. cultural

## IV. Trying the Translation
### Section A
1. 在集市上,张明山仔细观察各行各业的人,以及地方戏中的各种角色。
2. 彩塑泥人《蒋门神》是他的代表作。
3. 张明山的作品表现了弃恶扬善的意愿。
4. 在慈禧太后60大寿时,地方官把一套大型手捏戏文泥人《蟠桃会》供奉内廷。
5. 泥塑艺术早已走出国门,成为中外文化交流的使者,为越来越多的国家和人民所接受和珍爱。

### Section B
1. These cars art being produced on a large scale.
2. The bomb could be set off at any time.
3. Both parts should observe the terms of a contract.
4. The government has recently initiated a massive new house building programme.
5. Is a questionnaire answered by 500 people truly representative of national opinion?

## V. Organizing Your Ideas
c    e    d    a    f    b

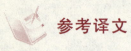

## 参考译文

### 泥 塑

民间艺人用天然的或廉价的材料,能够做出精美小巧的工艺品,博得民众的喜爱。其中最著名的是天津的"泥人张"和江苏无锡的惠山泥人。

"泥人张"是北方流传的一派民间彩塑,它创始于清代末年。"泥人张"创始人叫张明山,生于天津,家境贫寒,从小跟父亲以捏泥人为业,养家糊口。张明山心灵手巧,富于想象,在集市上,张明山仔细观察各行各业的人,以及地方戏中的各种角色,偷偷地在袖口里捏制。他捏制出来的泥人栩栩如生,逼真传神,一时蜚声中外,老百姓都喜爱他的作品,亲切地送给他一个昵称:泥人张。

彩塑泥人《蒋门神》是他的代表作,非常传神。蒋门神泥人像只有11厘米,人头不过蚕豆大小,但这个有个性的人物却被生动地呈现在读者眼前。只见这个恶棍,双手背在身后,蛮横地腆着肚皮,一副霸悍相,他如同一头狰狞的怪兽,随时随地都可能向人施发狂暴。青筋露起的脖颈,满脸杀气,眉目上挑,嘴角下撇,一个恶霸被刻画得淋漓尽致。张明山善于在泥塑中运用绘画技巧,使泥塑单纯雅致,富于装饰趣味,作品透出一种明快清新的气息,也表现了弃恶扬善的道德意义。

江苏无锡的惠山泥人历史悠久,与泥人张的风格完全不同。在这里,一到农闲季节,几乎家家都做泥人。每逢过年,在庙会和集市上,人们到处叫卖自己做的泥人。彩塑师王春林制作五盘泥孩儿进献,得到清代乾隆皇帝的赞赏。清同治到光绪年间,是惠山泥人历史上最昌盛的时期。这一时期,惠山有作坊、店铺40多家,专业匠师30多人。在慈禧太后60大寿时,地方官把一套大型手捏戏文泥人《蟠桃会》供奉内廷,从此惠山泥人成为贡品。

惠山泥人有粗货、细货之分。惠山泥人造型矮小,夸大头部,着重刻画表情。常用的色彩有大红、绿、金黄、青等原色,使惠山泥人鲜明艳丽,赏心悦目。

泥塑艺术是中华民族民间艺术的一种,它早已走出国门,成为中外文化交流的使者,为越来越多的国家和人民所接受和珍爱。

## TEXT B

# NEW YEAR'S WOOD BLOCK PAINTINGS

## Background Information

1. **Spring Festival** The most important and biggest festival in China. To the Chinese people it is as important as Christmas to people in the West. It is the first day of the lunar calendar and usually occurs somewhere between January 30 and February 20, heralding the beginning of spring, thus it is known as Spring Festival. This traditional festival is also a festival of

reunion, thus no matter how far away people are from their home, they would try their best to get back home to have the Reunion Dinner.

2. **New Year's Wood Block Paintings**　　Wood block printing was invented in the Song Dynasty and made the production of New Year's Wood Block Paintings much easier. As this art form developed and became more and more popular among Chinese people, its content and functions also increased. The content of New Year paintings were enriched later to depict Chinese farmers' life and Chinese folk stories and tales, which made Chinese peasants life more colorful and enhanced their knowledge.

　　It reached a peak in the Qing Dynasty. The painting draft is first engraved on wood and then printed, or the outline of the painting engraved and printed and then the blanks are filled with pens.

　　There are many types of New Year's Wood Block Paintings. The Gate Gods are pasted on doors and, according to their roles; there are the main gate god, secondary gate god, back gate god and wing room gate god. There are also New Year's Wood Block Paintings of the God of Stove and the God of Wealth. At Spring Festival time, New Year engravings of various types are put in every corner of the room and courtyard, imparting a strong festival atmosphere.

　　As time went on, the backward and superstitious content of New Year pictures gradually disappeared, but the style was preserved as a popular art form. Over the past five decades, Chinese folk artists have created some new wood engraving forms to portray reality. In the 1950s and 1960s, New Year's Wood Block Paintings became very popular among the people, and new printing technologies were adopted to speed printing and increase the number of copies. Until now, no other painting form has achieved a larger publishing volume than New Year's Wood Block Paintings.

3. **Yangjiabu New Year Picture**　　It originated in Weifang County, Shandong Province. This type of folk woodblock picture is produced in the workshops situated in Yangjiabu and Longchang. It flourished at the beginning of the Qianlong Period of the Qing Dynasty. Influenced by Yangliuqing New Year picture at the outset, it had a distinctive style later. Its thematic sources are from the Males' Ten Businesses, the Females' Ten Businesses, Lord Bao's Taking Office, Kongming's Town-Emptying Plot, etc.

4. **Taohuawu Prints of Suzhou**　　Suzhou was once the most prosperous region of the Chinese Empire. In addition to the region's economic prosperity, it also produced scores of Chinese intellectuals and artists. Beginning in the 16th century, Taohuawu woodblock printing played an integral role in this area's cultural heritage and history.

5. **Puhui New Year Painting**　　It originated by the Wang in Gaomi. At the early of the Ming Dynasty, Pupui Year Painting had won great reputation. Then the technique is excellent. Craft has charm. Experts praise that Puhui Year Painting is the strange flower of Folks Art.

## Language Points

1. **approach**  *v.*  to come near or nearer to (sb/sth) in space or time

    As I approached the house, I noticed a light on upstairs.

    She heard footsteps approaching.

    I moved out of the way as the procession approached.

    We approached the house.

2. **atmosphere**  *n.* [sing.]  feeling in the mind that is created by a group of people or a place; mood

    An atmosphere of optimism dominated the conference.

    The castle was centuries old and full of atmosphere.

    The atmosphere at home was rather tense.

3. **ward sb/sth off**  to keep away (sb/sth that is dangerous or unpleasant); to fend sb/sth off

    Don't forget insect repellent to ward off the mosquitoes.

    I've managed to ward off a cold this winter by taking these tablets.

4. **origin**  *n.* [C, U]  starting-point; source

    The origins of the custom are unknown.

    He is a German by origin.

    The tradition has its origins in the Middle Ages.

5. **repel**  *v.*  to drive (sb/sth) back or away; repulse

    The army was ready to repel an attack.

    The surface repels moisture, ie. does not allow it to penetrate.

6. **peak**  *n.* [C, U]  point of highest intensity, value, achievement, etc.

    Traffic reaches a peak between 8 and 9 in the morning.

    She's at the peak of her career.

    Sales have reached a new peak.

    The Kenyan runner was at his peak in the 1989 Games.

7. **add to sth**  to increase sth

    The house has been added to new rooms from time to time.

    The rise in electricity costs has added to the lack of money.

    This show will no doubt add to his growing reputation.

8. **bless**  *v.*  to ask God's favor and protection for (sb/sth)

    The villagers blessed the harvest.

    They brought the children to Jesus and he blessed them.

    The priest blessed the ship before it left port.

9. **appreciate**  *v.*  to understand and enjoy (sth); to value highly

    I'm not an expert, but I appreciate fine works of art.

    They don't appreciate good wine.

    You can't fully appreciate foreign literature in translation.

10. **outline**  *n. [C, U]*   line(s) showing the shape or outer edge (of sth)

   She could see only the outline(s) of the trees in the dim light.

   He draws an outline map of Italy.

   The outline of animals was cut into the rock.

11. **in addition (to sb/sth)**   as an extra person, thing or circumstance

   Candidates should fill in and return the form. In addition, they should enclose a recent, passport-size photograph.

   In addition to giving a general introduction to computers, the course also provides practical experience.

   In addition (to the names on the list) there are six other applicants.

   In addition to his movie work, Redford is known as a champion of environmental causes.

12. **originate**  *v.*   to have sth/sb as a cause or beginning

   A lot of our medicines originate from tropical plants.

   The idea originated with the ancient Greek philosophers.

   The town originated as a small fishing port.

13. **flourish**  *v.*   to develop quickly and be successful, very active, or widespread; prosper

   No new business can flourish in the present economic climate.

   The company has really flourished since we moved our factory to Scotland.

   The economy is booming and small businesses are flourishing.

14. **adopt**  *v.*   to take over and have or use (sth) as one's own

   The courts were asked to adopt a more flexible approach to young offenders.

   The store recently adopted a drug testing policy for all new employees.

   California has adopted a tough stance on the issue.

15. **integrate**  *v.*   to combine sth in such a way that it becomes fully a part of sth else

   We need to integrate these findings with the results of previous research.

   The buildings and the landscape are well integrated.

   We integrate private schools into the state education system.

# Answer Keys

## I. Getting the Message

### Section A

1. Y   2. N   3. N   4. N   5. N   6. NG

### Section B

1. on walls and doors

2. ward off the hosts

3. express people's New Year wishes and blessings

4. the invention of modern printing technology

5. folk woodblock picture
6. after the image appears

## II. Recognizing Main Ideas

1. pasted   2. Spring Festival   3. invented   4. Dynasty   5. decorate
6. enriched   7. depict   8. tales   9. enhanced   10. achieved

参考译文

# 木版年画

  年画,顾名思义,就是过年(春节)时张贴的画。旧时候,每逢春节来临,新的一年即将到来的时候,家家户户都把房院打扫得干干净净,在窗旁、门上、墙上以及灶前贴上焕然一新的年画,既用以创造喜气洋洋的新年气氛,又借以祈求上天赐给幸福,消除灾祸与不幸。

  古书里记载,传说很久以前,有名叫神荼、郁垒的两个兄弟,专门监督百鬼,发现有害的鬼就捆绑起来去喂老虎。于是黄帝就在门户上画神荼、郁垒的像用以防鬼。后来"门神"画产生的缘由还有一种说法,据说唐代皇帝曾命吴道子画钟馗像,并摹刻出来分赏给大臣贴挂以避鬼。随着年画的广泛流传,其内容和功能也不断丰富。到清代,年画发展到高峰。从最初被作为避邪驱鬼的符录,渐渐地又增加了题材,从而也具有表达人们对新一年的美好祝愿。

  民间年画基本上属于农民自己的艺术。画中形象自然、简练单纯,比较直白地表达农民朴实的主观愿望。很多画面都有装饰性、趣味性,色彩鲜艳强烈。这样的表现方法既适合于广大农民、市民的欣赏习惯和审美趣味,也便于木板印刷制作。民间年画是先画出底稿,再复刻在木板上印刷而成,或印出轮廓线,再用笔填色。在现代印刷技术产生之前,这是大批量生产图画的唯一方法。而且民间木版年画也有很多种。

**绵竹年画**

  绵竹年画与天津杨柳青、山东潍坊杨家埠、苏州桃花坞齐名为中国四大年画之一。它是流行于中国西南的年画品种,产于四川省绵竹县,兴于明末清初,盛行于清代。生产过程是先印墨版,再敷彩。

**杨柳青年画**

  杨柳青年画始创于明代崇祯年间天津市西杨柳青镇,清代雍正、乾隆年间是年画发展的鼎盛时期。采用木版套印和手工彩绘相结合的方法,在墨线版刷印出形象后,再由人工敷彩上色。人物脸面和衣饰多以铅粉、金色晕染。题材多样,深为广大人民群众所喜爱。

**朱仙镇木版年画**

  朱仙镇木版年画距今已有800多年的历史,是我国最古老的民间艺术精华之一。在当地其制作多沿用旧法。

# Reading in Focus

## 英语长、难句的阅读 Understand Long Sentences (2)

插入成分,作为英语的一项特殊语法项,属于独立成分的一种,同句子中的其他部分只有意义上的联系,而没有语法上的联系,将其删掉后,句子结构仍然完整。插入成分通常由一个词、一个短语或一个句子构成,可以表示说话人对所说内容所持的态度、看法,或对所说的话进行解释,也可以用来联系两个句子或两个段落,表示上下文之间存在的关系,如表示顺序、转换话题、表示总结、让步、对立等。插入成分的位置,可放在句首、句中或句末,一般可置于两个逗号、两个破折号之间或一个破折号之后,或置于圆括号或中括号里,或置于冒号之后,也有不用任何标点符号标明的插入成分。除了同位语,非限定性定语从句之外,还有其他的表现形式可以作插入成分。

下面从它的位置,表现形式以及表意功能(作用)方面介绍插入成分。

**关于插入成分的位置**

(一) 一般说来,插入成分在句中的位置比较灵活,可置于句首或句中,也可置于句末,如下面例句中表强调、推断等的 surely:

1. **Surely** you don't believe that!
2. You **surely** don't mean to be cruel.
3. You don't want to hurt his feelings, **surely**!

当然,并不是所有的插入语都是有这三种位置。例如,有的只可置于句首,有的只可置于句末,而且常用逗号将其与句子主体部分分开。例如:

1. (误) Have you **talking of football**, seen the Indian team play?
2. (误) Have you seen the Indian team play, **talking of the football**?
3. (正) **Talking of football**, have you seen the Indian team play?

(二) 插入成分也可置于两个逗号、两个破折号之间或一个破折号之后,或置于圆括或中括里,或置于冒号之后。例如:

1. All of them, **nevertheless**, insist upon continuing the experiment.
2. If you are wrong—**and I am sure you are in the wrong**—you must apologize.
3. Miss Jane (**She is Mrs. John now**) is here.
4. There comes a bus [**made in Shanghai**]—**very beautiful**—filled with many passengers.

(三) 也有不用任何标点符号标明插入成分位置的,往往不容易识别出来。例如:

Who **do you think** is the best singer in your class?

关于插入成分的表现形式

| 表现形式 | 常用示例 | 例句 |
|---|---|---|
| 形容词，形容词加不定式或形容词引起的词组 | sorry, true, wonderful, excellent, worst still, needless to say, strange to say, sure enough, most important of all, etc. | *Wonderful*, our team has won again.<br>*Strange to say*, she hasn't got my letter up to now.<br>*Most important of all*, we should trust and support each other. |
| 副词或副词短语 | generally, personally, fortunately, furthermore, otherwise, indeed, however, anyway, sure enough, firstly, undoubtedly, nevertheless, etc. | He was, *indeed*, an optimist.<br>He said he would come, and *sure enough* he did come.<br>When he got to England, he found, *however*, that his English was too limited. |
| 介词短语<br>in-phrases,<br>for-phrases,<br>by-phrases,<br>as-phrases,<br>at-phrases,<br>on-phrases,<br>to-phrases 等 | in one's view, in reality, in theory;<br>for example, for the first time;<br>by the way, by all accounts, by comparison;<br>as a matter of fact, as usual;<br>at least, at worst, at any rate;<br>to one's mind, to a man, etc. | *In my opinion*, he's not right.<br>You cannot depend on her; *for instance*, she arrived late for an important meeting yesterday.<br>This one is really cheaper *by comparison*.<br>*As a matter of fact*, I was the one who broke the glass.<br>It's going to be warmer tomorrow—*at least*, so the weather forecast says.<br>He is, *on the whole*, a satisfactory student.<br>*To my mind*, he's a kind person. |
| 不定式短语 | to be (more) exact, to be brief, to be sure, to make/cut a long story short, to tell the truth, to be precise, to conclude, etc. | *To cut a long story short,* they thought it more economical to live in the country.<br>There were thirty people present, *to be precise*.<br>*To tell you the truth*, I'm not so interested in the matter. |
| 现在分词短语 | generally speaking, judging from, considering, allowing for, etc. | *Judging from* what you say, he ought to have come earlier.<br>*Generally speaking*, his work is satisfactory. |
| 分句,从句 | I am sure, I believe, I'm afraid, it is said, as we know, believe it or not, what is worse, if you don't mind, etc. | He said nothing, and *what is worse*, laughed at us.<br>*I believe*, China will catch up with the developed countries sooner or later. |
| 名词(相当于同位语) | | England, *the largest country in Britain*, is in the southeast of this land.<br>Beijing, *the capital of China*, is a beautiful city. |

**关于插入成分的表意功能(作用)**                                                                 续表

| 表意功能 | 例 句 |
|---|---|
| 表示说话者的态度看法 | It was late in getting to the station, *but fortunately for me*, the train was late too. |
| 表示说话者的估计和推测 | It will result in success, *I suppose*. |
| 表示补充说明 | He left there last year, *that is to say*, in 2007. |
| 表引起对方注意、观察或思考 | New York, *as you know*, is situated on the Hudson River. |
| 表示肯定或强调 | I am not guessing — *I really know*. |
| 表示列举 | We now need two hours to think about that, *say*, from four to six. |
| 表示顺序 | You should give him some help. *In the first place,* send her for a doctor. *In the second place*, send him some money. |
| 表示话题转换 | *By the way*, have you finished your homework? |
| 表示增补或引申 | The task is very difficult, *besides*, time presses.<br>He rejected my command, *and what is more*, insulted me before the whole company. |
| 表示概括或总结 | *In a word / To sum up*, don't get swollen headed because of victory. |
| 表示转折或对立 | It's very cold; he didn't wear his overcoat *though*.<br>Why do you think we cannot pass the exam? *On the contrary*, we can. |
| 表示让步或委婉语气 | *Anyhow*, she has so far overcome all the difficulties.<br>You'll get caught in the rain, *I am afraid*. |
| 表示结果或等同 | They didn't listen to the teacher in class. *As a result*, they failed examination.<br>My brother was taught by mother, *and similarly*, so was I. |
| 表示时间的过渡 | Tom was now undergoing many hardships. His brother *in the meantime* was having an easy time. |

# EXERCISES

**I. Direction: Analyze the underlined parts which are complicated, and tell how complicated they are. Then write down their grammatical functions they have in the brackets.**

1. The most famous were <u>the Clay Figurine Zhang made in Tianjin and the Huishan clay figurines made in Wuxi, Jiangsu Province.</u>
   表语(平行结构做表语,带有 v-ed 做后置定语)

2. When Empress Dowager Cixi celebrated her 60th birthday, the local officer of Huishan presented <u>a clay figurine set, Immortality Peach Gathering.</u>
   宾语(带有同位语)

3. It is said that, in the Tang Dynasty, the emperor asked Wu Daozi to draw Zhong Kui and
　　分句做插入成分
　　Reproduce it to send to his officials to repel evil.
4. In addition and there are many types of New Year's Wood Block Paintings.
　　介词短语做插入成分
5. There comes a bus [made in Shanghai]—very beautiful—filled with many passengers.
　　插入成分　　　　　　插入成分

**II. Direction: Translate the following groups of sentences into English and analyze how a long or complicated sentence is formed.**

1. I went to Beijing last week.
　　↪ I went to Beijing, a beautiful city, last week.
　　　　↪ I went to Beijing, a beautiful city, which is the capital of China last week.
2. Everyone must obey the rules.
　　↪ Everyone in the company must obey the rules.
　　　　↪ Everyone in the company, whether men or women, must obey the rules.
3. A satellite is an object.
　　↪ A satellite is an object, which travels in an orbit round another object in space.
　　　　↪ A satellite is an object, either natural or man-made, which travels in an orbit round another object in space.
4. He rang up all his friends.
　　↪ He rang up all his friends in the pop world.
　　　　↪ He rang up all his friends in the pop world, including the most famous pop stars.
5. I enjoy learning new things.
　　↪ I enjoy learning new things from politics to sports and music.
　　　　↪ In addition, I enjoy learning new things from politics to sports and music.

# Hip-hop Culture

 ## Script for Lead-in Listening

Listen to the following conversation and fill in the blanks with the correct words or phrases. You may choose the words or phrases from the list given.

**Anchor:** Hello, Mike, have you ever heard of "hip-hop"?

**Mike:** Yeah sure. When I was a kid in the Bronx, I could buy hip-hop CDs from guys on the street. To me, hip-hop then was everywhere. One of the first songs that really spoke to me was Jay-Z's "Hard Knock Life".

**Anchor:** What was it about then?

**Mike:** He talked about growing up in the ghetto. The (music) video looked like where I'm from. I felt like I understood what he was saying.

**Anchor:** Yes. People often say that hip-hop is where they get to express what and who they are and where they come from.

**Mike:** But when I got older, some hip-hop lyrics began to trouble me. I was disappointed at what I was hearing, in terms of images and music... it was degrading.

**Anchor:** I can understand that. Rappers are sending a lot of different messages. As a teenager, you're going through a lot, but if hip-hop is your main source of information, and it's dumbing down and you don't have a great education to begin with, it's destructive.

**Mike:** So that's why my mom's so concerned about what I'm listening to... Now I listen to the rappers who are promoting positive things and I also like less well-known up-and-coming rappers.

**Anchor:** So what do you think of people's criticism of hip-hop in general?

**Mike:** I know that people tend to criticize hip-hop for offensive content and maybe hip-hop needs to change there. Rappers should use it as a tool, rather than a weapon. But hip-hop is a mirror, a reflection of society at large.

## NEW WORDS AND EXPRESSIONS IN LEAD-IN LISTENING

**lyrics**　　*n.*　　the words of a song

**degrade**　　*adj.*　　treating sb as if they have no value, so that they lose their self-respect and the respect of other people

**offensive**　　*adj.*　　(*formal*) extremely unpleasant; [only before noun] connected with that act of attacking sb/sth

**promote** *v.* to help sth to happen or develop

**reflection** *n. [C]* (BrE also less frequent **reflexion**) a sign that shows the state or nature of sth

**dumb down** to make sth less educational, and of worse quality, by trying to make is easier for people to understand

**be concerned about** worried and feeling concern about sth 担心的；忧虑的

**criticize sth for** to say that you disapprove of sb/sth because of...

# NOT MERELY MUSIC: THE PHENOMENON OF HIP-HOP

 ## Background Information

1. **Hip-Hop** Cultural movement that attained widespread popularity in the 1980s and 1990s; also, the backing music for rap, the musical style incorporating rhythmic and/or rhyming speech that became the movement's most lasting and influential art form.

   Although widely considered a synonym for rap music, the term hip-hop refers to a complex culture comprising four elements: deejaying, or "turntabling"; rapping, also known as "MCing" or "rhyming"; graffiti painting, also known as "graffiti" or "writing"; and "B-boying", which encompasses hip-hop dance, style, and attitude, along with the sort of virile body language that philosopher Cornel West described as "postural semantics". Hip-hop originated in the predominantly African American, economically depressed South Bronx section of New York City in the late 1970s. As the hip-hop movement began at society's margins, its origins are shrouded in myth, enigma, and obfuscation.

2. **Hip-Hop Dance** A kind of popular dance to the music with a regular heavy beat and spoken words.

3. **Rap** A type of popular music which the words of a song are sung, but spoken in time to music with a steady beat.

4. **DJ(Disk Jockey)** A person who conducts a program of recorded music on radio, on television, or at discotheques or other dance halls. Disc jockey programs became the economic base of many radio stations in the United States after World War II. The format generally involves one person, the disc jockey, introducing and playing phonograph records and chatting informally and usually extemporaneously in the intervals.

   The idea of the program originated in the 1930s, but its development was hampered by a Federal Communications Commission rule that required stations to identify recorded music frequently—so frequently, as it turned out, that the message tended to irritate and alienate the listener. The disc jockey was also restricted by musicians and artists whose phonograph labels bore the warning "Not Licensed for Radio Broadcast." But the show's potential was revealed when Martin Block broadcast his *Make Believe Ballroom* on station WNEW in New York City as filler between news coverage of the closely followed trial of the kidnapper of the Charles A. Lindbergh baby. Upon the request of thousands of listeners, the makeshift show was retained by the station after the kidnap trial. In 1940 the Federal Communications Commission relaxed its rules, requiring that recorded material be identified only twice in an hour, and in the same year the courts ruled that the warning on record labels had no legal significance. From that time disc jockey shows became increasingly popular.

The radio disc jockey's future was clouded again during World War II by industry wage disputes with the American Society of Composers, Authors, and Publishers (ASCAP) and the American Federation of Musicians. At issue was the declining demand for live appearances of artists because of the popularity of disc jockeys and recorded music. In 1944 the disputes were settled, and wartime controls on vinylite and shellac, the materials from which phonograph records were made, were eased.

By the 1950s listener loyalty to disc jockeys was so firmly established that the success of any record depended on the preferences of the disc jockey. To solicit their favour, record companies began to shower the disc jockeys with money, stocks, or gifts (commonly known as payola). This widespread practice of commercial bribery was given national exposure by a federal investigation in 1959. As a result, payola faded for a while, but in the mid-1980s new exposés revealed that the practice continued to exist in many quarters.

The disc jockey format was never as popular on television as on radio, with the exception of a few dance shows.

5. **MC**   the person in a rap group who holds the microphone and says the words to the songs.
6. **DJ Kool Herc**   The father of the breakbeat, the deejay practice of isolating and repeating "breaks", the most danceable portions of songs; breakbeats make up the foundation of modern hip-hop.

## Language Points

1. **element**   *n.*   a necessary or typical part of sth
    *The story has all the elements of a soap opera.*
    *Customer relations is an important element of the job.*
2. **spin**   *v.*   (spinning, spun, spun) to turn round and round quickly
    *a spinning ice skater*
    *My head is spinning(= I feel as if my head is going around and I can't balance).*
3. **acrobatic**   *adj.*   involving or performing difficult acts or movements with the body
    *acrobatic feats*
    *an acrobatic dancer*
4. **percussion**   *n. [U]*   a. musical instruments that are played by being struck by the hand or by an object such as a stick or hammer, especially as a division(percussion section) of a band;

b. (the effect or sound produced by) the forceful striking together of two hard objects

   percussion instruments

   The track features Joey Langton on percussion.

5. **origin**　*n.*　the point from which sth starts; the cause of sth

   the origins of life on earth

   Most coughs are viral in origin(= caused by a virus).

   The origin of the word remains obscure.

6. **ingenuity**　*n.* [U]　the ability to invent things or solve problems in clever new ways

   The problem tested the ingenuity of even the most imaginative students.

7. **ghetto**　*n.* [pl. ~os or ~oes]　an area of a city where many people of the same race or background live, separately from the rest of the population. Ghettos are often crowded, with bad living conditions

   a poor kid growing up in the ghetto

8. **immigrate**　*v.*　(especially AmE)　to come and live permanently in a country after leaving your own country

   About 6.6 million people immigrated to the US in the 1970s.

9. **infectious**　*adj.*　capable of causing infection

   Flu is highly infectious.

   (figurative) infectious laughter

10. **inspire**　*v.*　to give sb the desire, confidence or enthusiasm to do sth well

    His superb play inspired the team to a thrilling 5-0 win.

    The actors inspired the kids with their enthusiasm.

11. **hard-core**　*adj.*　having a belief or a way of be having that will not change

    hard-core party members

    four hard-core leaders of the gang

12. **verbal**　*adj.*　relating to words

    The job applicant must have good verbal skills.

    non-verbal communication(= gestures, expressions of the face, etc.)

13. **gymnastics**　*n.* [U]　physical exercises that develop and show the body's strength and ability to move and bend easily, often done as a sport in competitions

    a gymnastics competition

    (figurative) mental/verbal gymnastics(=quick or clever thinking or use of words)

14. **band**　*n.*　a group of musicians, especially a group that play popular music

    a rock/jazz band

    a military band

    She's a singer with a band.

15. **fad**　*n.*　something that people are interested in for only a short period of time

    the latest/current fad

    a fad for physical fitness

    Rap music proved to be more than just a passing fad.

16. **There is no denying (the fact) that**

    There is no denying (the fact) that quicker action could have saved them.

17. **signs of...**   an event, an action, a fact, etc. that shows that sth exists, is happening or may happen in the future

    Headaches may be a sign of stress.

    Her work is showing some signs of improvement.

    There was no sign of life in the house(= there seemed to be nobody there).

18. **along with**   sb/sth in addition to sb/sth; in the same way as sb/sth

    There was a bill along with the parcel.

    She placed bank notes, along with the change, back to the drawer.

19. **be short on sth**   not enough

    He was a big strapping guy but short on brains.

    The country is badly short on wheat.

20. **regard sb/sth as sth**   to think about sb/sth in a particular way

    Capital punishment was regarded as inhuman and immoral.

    He regards himself as a patriot.

    She is widely regarded as the current leader's natural successor.

21. **attribute sth to sth**   to say or believe that sth is the result of a particular thing

    She attributes her success to hard work and a little luck.

    He attributed blame for the failure to his colleague.

22. **a flash in the pan**   a sudden success that lasts only a short time and is not likely to be repeated

    She did pass one exam but it was just a flash in the pan.

    The wonderful book is just a flash in the pan; he can never write another.

# Answer Keys

## I. Getting the Message

1. D    2. C    3. D    4. B    5. B

## II. Developing Your Vocabulary

### Section A

1. infecious    2. element    3. spun    4. inspired    5. fad    6. verbal

### Section B

1. attributes/attributed    2. immigrated    3. regarded as

4. shows no sign of    5. rather than    6. have no idea

## III. Recognizing Main Ideas

1. becoming    2. among    3. type    4. cultural

5. including    6. originated    7. development    8. path

## IV. Trying the Translation

### Section A

1. 不管你对嘻哈音乐的看法怎么样，无可否认它已经对世界各地的通俗文化造成冲击，并且没有减弱的迹象。
2. 嘻哈风带来了一些专有术语。
3. 嘻哈文化起源于非洲传统的打击乐和口述故事。
4. 总的来说东岸风格是核心力量，说唱歌手拥护以非洲为中心观点的政治和社会理想。
5. 一度被视为昙花一现的嘻哈风，却决心继续走它的创造与赞美之路，带领更多的归附者上路。

### Section B

1. The plane was spinning out of control.
2. This particular custom has its origins in Africa.
3. The actors' enthusiasm inspired the kids.
4. She lost her job when the factory closed, along with hundreds of others.
5. He attributes her success to hard work.

## V. Organizing Your Ideas

b    d    e    f    a    c

参考译文

## 所向披靡嘻哈风

现在，从大众广播到电视广告，嘻哈音乐似乎无所不在。不管你对嘻哈音乐的看法怎么样，无可否认它已经对世界各地的通俗文化造成冲击，并且没有减弱的迹象。

嘻哈风带来了一些专有术语："说唱乐"是指配合节奏念文字的动作。"嘻哈"既是一种音乐，同时也是一种文化，嘻哈文化包含四大要素："MC"（随节奏说唱）、"DJ"（转动唱片及混音）、"霹雳舞"（一种特技般的舞蹈）和"涂鸦艺术"。除此之外嘻哈文化还有其他一些特殊的方面，如语言和服装时尚等。

嘻哈文化起源于非洲传统的打击乐和口述故事。然而，现代嘻哈则是20世纪70年代初期来源于纽约市犯罪行为猖獗的南布朗克斯区。那些口袋空空却富于创新的年轻人，厌倦了当时流行的乏味的迪斯科音乐，便创出了一种新的动感十足的艺术形式：通过配合节奏念词的方式，在言辞上相互较量，并且记录了贫民区的生活。

被公认为嘻哈之父的库尔·贺克是牙买加人，他是12岁移民到纽约的。1973年左右，他开始在布朗克斯区的家庭宴会中担任DJ。在他主持的节奏布鲁斯、灵歌和方舞等极富感染力的节目里，他还加入了"toasting"（对群众说话）和"dub talk"（跟着拍子有节奏地讲话）等

44

牙买加风俗节目。

培养嘻哈文化的正面力量要归功于曾做过帮派头目和 DJ 的阿弗里卡·班巴塔，他被公认为嘻哈文化的教父。他不仅努力把迅速发展的嘻哈音乐团体团结起来，而且还激励帮派份子在说唱和霹雳舞上进行创造性的互相较量，而不是通过暴力。

20 世纪 80 年代，随着嘻哈风更加盛行，新的流派发展起来。总的来说东岸风格是核心力量，说唱歌手拥护以非洲为中心观点的政治和社会理想。西岸的嘻哈风主要是帮派份子的说唱，充满了关于帮派、枪支和不可避免的街头生活等内容。西岸风格引起了更多群众的兴趣而为之激动，所以在都市和近郊地区都很受欢迎。

尽管有些嘻哈迷抱怨说，现在的嘻哈文化中，原有的锐气和政治信息已经没有了，但这种类型仍在不断扩展、革新并且发挥其影响力。在它短暂的历史中，嘻哈文化从仅有两个唱机转盘发展到了混音器和现场演奏的乐手；从四拍子的说唱到越来越复杂的嘴上功夫；从南布朗克斯的发祥地到世界的每个角落。

东岸嘻哈乐团"Run DMC"中的罗恩曾说：在有些人称嘻哈只是一种时尚时，他们根本不了解它背后的热情。一度被视为昙花一现的嘻哈风，却决心继续走它的创造与赞美之路，带领更多的归附者上路。

## WHAT IS HIP-HOP TO ME

## Language Points

1. **a student of something**   to be very interested in a particular subject

    *Vivien is a student of music.*

    *He's obviously an excellent student of human nature.*

2. **on occasion**   sometimes but not often

    *They visit New York on occasion.*

    *On occasion prisoners were allowed visits from their families.*

3. **intimate**   *a.* having an extremely close friendship

    *an intimate friend*

    *an intimate relationship*

4. **inform**   *v.* to formally or officially tell someone about something or give them information

    *Please inform us of any change of address as soon as possible.*

    *We regret to inform you that your application has been rejected.*

    *They decided to inform the police.*

5. **be conscious of**   to be aware of

    *He was very conscious of security.*

    *She is really conscious of her health.*

6. **used to**   a. if something used to happen, it happened regularly or all the time in the past, but does not happen now

   *He used to go to our school.*

   *We're eating out more often than we used to.*

   **used not to do sth** (British English)

   *You used not to fuss like this.*

   b. if a particular situation used to exist, it existed for a period of time in the past, but does not exist now

   *Jimmy used to be a friend of mine.*

   *There used to be a large car park on this site.*

   **not use to be/do sth**

   *Why are you so bad-tempered? You didn't use to be like this.*

   **sb/sth use to be/do sth**

   *Did this building use to be a hotel?*

   *Where did you use to live before you came to Manchester?*

7. **save up**   to keep money in a bank so that you can use it later, especially when you gradually add more money over a period of time

   *You should save some money up, instead of spending it.*

8. **rhyme**   *n. [c]*   a. a word that has the same sound or ends with the same sound as another word

   *Can you think of a rhyme for "moon"?*

   b. a short poem in which the last word in the line has the same sound as the last word in another line

   *Children's rhymes and stories*

   *v.*   a. if two words or lines of poetry rhyme, they end with the same sound, including a vowel

   *"Hat" rhymes with "cat".*

   *The song has rhyming couplets (=pairs of lines that end in words that rhyme).*

   b. to put two or more words together to make them rhyme

   *You can't rhyme "box" with "backs".*

9. **pursue**   *v.*   a. to continue doing an activity or trying to achieve something over a long period of time

   *She plans to pursue a career in politics.*

   *Students should pursue their own interests, as well as do their school work.*

   **pursue a goal/aim/objective, etc.**

   *companies that pursue the traditional goal of profits*

   *a campaign promise to pursue policies that will help the poor*

   **pursue the matter/argument/question, etc.**   to continue trying to find out about or persuade someone about a particular subject

   *Janet did not dare pursue the matter further.*

   *The defence pursued the question of Dr Carrington's state of mind.*

   b. to chase or follow someone or something, in order to catch them, attack them, etc.

*Briggs ran across the field with one officer pursuing him.*

   c. to keep trying to persuade someone to have a relationship with you

   *I was pleased, but somewhat embarrassed, when she pursued me.*

10. **be opposed to sth**   to disagree with sth such as a plan or system

    *Most of us are opposed to the death penalty.*

    *Two ideas that are opposed to each other are completely different from each other.*

    *The principles of capitalism and socialism are diametrically opposed (=completely opposite).*

    **as opposed to sth**   used to compare two things and show that they are different from each other

    *Students discuss ideas, as opposed to just copying from books.*

11. **stardom**   the state of being a famous performer

    *his rapid rise to stardom*

    **shoot/rise/zoom to stardom**   become famous very quickly

    *Ellen shot to stardom as a model last year.*

12. **decent**   *a.*   a. [usually before noun] of a good enough standard or quality

    *a decent salary*

    *a house with a decent-sized yard*

    *Don't you have a decent jacket?*

    *Their in-flight magazine is actually halfway decent (=quite good).*

    b. following moral standards that are acceptable to society

    *decent citizens/people/folk, etc.*

    *a decent burial*

    *Paul visited the local bars more frequently than was decent for a senior lecturer.*

    *The chairman did the decent thing (=did what people thought he ought to) and resigned.*

    c. [usually before noun] treating people in a fair and kind way

    *I decided her father was a decent guy after all. It was decent of you to show up today.*

    d. wearing enough clothes so that you do not show too much of your body—used humorously

    *Are you decent? Can I come in?*

13. **mainstream**   *n.*   the most usual ideas or methods, or the people who have these ideas or methods

    *Environmental ideas have been absorbed into the mainstream of European politics.*

    *Genet started as a rebel, but soon became part of the literary mainstream.*

14. **integrity**   *n.*   a. the quality of being honest and strong about what you believe to be right

    *personal/professional/political, etc. integrity*

    *a man of great moral integrity*

    b. formal the state of being united as one complete thing

    *the territorial integrity of the country*

15. **matter**   *v.*   a. [not in progressive] to be important, especially to be important to you, or to have an effect on what happens

    **it doesn't etc. matter if**

*Will it matter if I'm a little late?*

*If I have to stay late at work tonight, it won't matter because we can go out another night.*

**it doesn't etc. matter who/why/what, etc.**

*It doesn't matter what you wear, as long as you look neat and tidy.*

*Does it matter what I think?*

**it doesn't, etc. matter that**

*It does not matter that the gun was in fact unloaded.*

*Do you think it matters that the cups and saucers don't match?*

**it doesn't matter about sth**

*Just give me $5—it doesn't matter about the rest.*

**matter to**

*He had lost many of the people who mattered to him.*

**matter a lot/a great deal**

*It mattered a great deal to her what other people thought of her.*

**matter much**

*I don't think it matters much what you study.*

**all that matters/the only thing that matters**

*All that matters is that you're safe.*

*Money was the only thing that mattered to him.*

**it doesn't matter** *(spoken)* a. used to tell someone that you are not angry or upset about something, especially something that they have done

*"I've spilled some coffee on the carpet."——"It doesn't matter."*

b. used to say that you do not mind which one of two things you have

*"Red or white wine?"——"Oh, either. It doesn't matter."*

**what does it matter?** *(spoken)* used to say that something is not important

*It all happened so long ago now, what does it matter?*

*What does it matter how old I am?*

16. **commercialize** *v.* a. [usually passive] to be more concerned with making money from something than about its quality—used to show disapproval

*Christmas has become so commercialized.*

b. to sell something completely new to the public for the first time

*Some space launches will be commercialized to help pay for more space research.*

17. **microcosm** *n.* a small group, society, or place that has the same qualities as a much larger one

**microcosm of**

*New York's mix of people is a microcosm of America.*

**in microcosm**

*All the problems of society can be seen here in microcosm.*

18. **individual** *a. & n.* a. [only before noun] considered separately from other people or things in the same group

*Each individual leaf on the tree is different.*
*the needs of the individual customer*

b. [only before noun] belonging to or intended for one person rather than a group
*Children get more individual attention in small classes.*
*You can have the bathroom designed to suit your individual needs.*

c. an individual style, way of doing things etc. is different from anyone else's—usually used to show approval

d. a person, considered separately from the rest of the group or society that they live in
*the rights of the individual*
*Each individual receives two genes, one inherited from each parent.*
*Most churches were built with donations from private individuals (=ordinary people, rather than the government or companies).*

e. a person of a particular kind, especially one who is unusual in some way
*a strange-looking individual*

19. **represent** *v.* a. to officially speak or take action for another person or group of people
*Mr Kobayashi was chosen to represent the company at the conference.*

b. to speak officially for someone in a court of law
*represent yourself*
*She decided to represent herself (=speak for herself without a lawyer) during the trial.*

c. [linking verb] to form or be something
*European orders represented 30 percent of our sales last year.*
*represent a change/an advance/an increase, etc.*

d. to have been elected to a parliament, council etc. by the people in a particular area
*He represents the Congressional District of Illinois.*

e. to be a sign or mark that means sth
*Brown areas represent deserts on the map.*

f. to be a symbol of sth
*He hated the school and everything it represented.*

g. if you represent your country, school, town etc in a sport, you take part in a sports event for that country, etc.
*Her greatest ambition was to represent her country at the Olympics.*

h. if a group, organization, area, etc. is represented at an event, people from it are at the event
*All the local clubs were represented in the parade.*

i. to describe someone or something in a particular way, esp. in a way that is not true
**represent sb/sth as sth**
*The article represents the millionaire as a simple family man.*
*He had represented himself as an employee in order to gain access to the files.*

j. if a painting, statue, piece of music, etc. represents sth or sb, it shows them
*Paintings representing religious themes were common in medieval times.*

20. **far from**   used to say that the opposite of sth is true, or the opposite of what you expect happens

   *far from wealthy and a comfortable life*
   *The struggle is far from over.*
   *Far from being kind, he was most cruel.*

21. **worship**   *n.&v.*   a. the activity of praying or singing in a religious building in order to show respect and love for a god

   *They bowed their heads in worship.*

   b. to show respect and love for a god, especially by praying in a religious building

   *They all worship the same god.*
   *a church where people have worshipped for hundreds of years*

   c. to admire and love someone very much

   *He absolutely worships her.*

   **worship the ground sb walks on**   to admire or love sb so much that you cannot see their faults

22. **for the sake of**   a. (also **for sb's/sth's sake**) in order to help, improve, or please sb or sth

   *He moved to the seaside for the sake of his health.*
   *I only went for Kay's sake.*
   *I hope he's told the truth for his own sake (=because it will be good for him).*

   b. **for God's/Christ's/goodness'/Heaven's, etc. sake** *(spoken)*

   1) used when you are telling sb how important it is to do sth or not to do sth

   *For goodness sake, don't be late!*

   2) used to show that you are angry or annoyed

   *What is it now, for God's sake?*

   c. **for the sake of it**   if you do sth for the sake of it, you do it because you want to and not for any particular reason

   *She likes spending money just for the sake of it.*

   d. **for its own sake**   (also **sth for sth's sake**) if sth is done for its own sake, it is done for the value of the experience itself, not for any advantage it will bring

   *art for art's sake*

   e. **for the sake of argument**   *(spoken)* if you say sth for the sake of argument, what you say may not be true but it will help you to have a discussion

   *Let's say, just for the sake of argument, that you've got £200 to invest.*

23. **comprise**   *v.*   a. to consist of particular parts, groups, etc.

   *The house comprises two bedrooms, a kitchen, and a living room.*

   **be comprised of sb/sth**

   *The committee is comprised of well-known mountaineers.*

   b. to form part of a larger group of people or things

   *Women comprise a high proportion of part-time workers.*

24. **confuse**  *v.*  a. to make sb feel that they cannot think clearly or do not understand

   *I understand the text but the diagrams are confusing me.*

   b. to think wrongly that a person or thing is sb or sth else

   *People might well confuse the two products.*

   **confuse sb/sth with sb/sth**

   *I always confuse you with your sister—you look so alike.*

   *Donald Regan, not to be confused with former President Ronald Reagan*

   **confuse the issue/matter/argument, etc.**  to make it even more difficult to think clearly about a situation or problem or to deal with it

   *He kept asking unnecessary questions which only confused the issue.*

25. **authentic**  *a.*  a. done or made in the traditional or original way

   *authentic French food*

   b. a painting, document, book etc. that is authentic has been proved to be by a particular person

   *authentic work by Picasso*

   c. based on facts

   *an authentic account*

   d. used to describe a copy that is the same as, or as good as, the original

   *Actors dressed in authentic costumes re-enact the battle.*

26. **comprehend**  *v.*  to understand sth that is complicated or difficult

   *She cannot comprehend the extent of the disaster.*

   *I did not fully comprehend what had happened.*

   **comprehend what/how/why, etc.**

   *It may be hard to comprehend how much this gift means for my country.*

   **comprehend that**

   *Finally, she comprehended that he wanted his pay.*

27. **in essence**  used when talking about the most basic and important part of something, esp. an idea, belief, or argument

   *In essence his message was very simple.*

   *Development of sicial economy is consistent with human being's development in essence.*

# Answer Keys

## I. Getting the Message

### Section A

1. N    2. Y    3. N    4. N    5. Y    6. NG

### Section B

1. he no longer financially supports hip-hop, nor he is necessarily inside the culture

2. it was an intimate part of his socialization

3. reality
4. far from a wealthy or a comfortable life
5. be a revolutionary art-form
6. are getting lost

## II. Recognizing Main Ideas

1. former  2. since  3. anymore  4. close  5. occasionally
6. pursue  7. reality  8. decent  9. evolved  10. mix

**参考译文**

## 我与嘻哈乐

　　我今年24岁，是个曾经对嘻哈乐很热衷的男生。之所以说是曾经热衷，是因为我现在不再用金钱来支撑我的嘻哈梦，也不像过去那样深陷其中难以自拔了。不过，我偶尔还会听听，毕竟它曾帮助我接触并且了解这个社会，是我成长过程中难以忘怀的一段经历。嘻哈乐（说唱）对我的言语表达也有很大的影响，那段日子想来真是对它痴迷，连睡梦中都感受得到它。我曾经张口成韵并做过DJ，相比之下我更擅长前者。我至今还记得曾经努力地攒下本来就不多的钱，只是为了买下一张密纹唱片，好让我能伴着器乐说唱。

　　后来我放弃了嘻哈乐，转而作出一心用功读书这一与我的明星梦相差甚远的选择，这并非因为缺乏音乐专业技巧、对梦想的追求或是缺少家人支持，最根本的原因在于我认识到了现实。我发现，要当一名嘻哈乐艺术家就需要把一生中几乎所有的时间和精力都倾注在唱片之类的事情当中，有时甚至需要牺牲个人的价值评判标准，否则就不会过上体面的生活。我知道主流文化圈内圈外很多人能够坚持自我的原则，但大多数身处圈外。可是，要是能不工作、不吃饭的话，我不想给别人留下"钱至关重要"的印象。我从不想使我自己商业化，或是看到音乐商业化，可是，我无能为力。

　　嘻哈文化如今成为社会文化的一个缩影，许多人因此而富有，但更多的嘻哈乐艺术家以及他们自称所代表的人一点都不富裕、生活更毫无舒适可言。我们陷入英雄崇拜和个人主义之中。强调个人成就赋予我们中的一些人智慧和独立——但是，这大多数情况下是通过牺牲很多而求得很少实现的。

　　我想，嘻哈乐现今的状况也就是构成这种文化的人们的真实状况。它曾经是一种革命性的艺术形式，而如今已毫无革命性可言。它只是略有变化，却没有实质上的发展。我们更多地把流行程度与唱片销售混为一谈，误认为是革新和创造。尽管Roots或Gangstarr乐队的唱片销售突破百万张，并不意味着他们如今就具有创造性。当我审视是究竟是谁在引导潮流，何为真正的嘻哈乐艺术时，我就不禁感到恐惧。

　　在对真实、创造、革新、时尚、流行和赢利的界定上我们正在迷失。人们总在谈论嘻哈文化，事实上却早已忘记了什么是嘻哈文化。今天的艺术家大都过于年轻，没有受过多少教育，甚至不能理解对我们的发展来说至关重要的那段历史。如果我们想把嘻哈文化继续下去的话，我只希望更多的人能真正的了解嘻哈。实际上，正是因此，我开始思考自己为什么曾经对嘻哈乐是那么的热衷。我和一些人一样，走着同样的路，也经受着同样的挣扎。

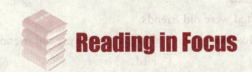

# Reading in Focus

## 英语长、难句的阅读 Understand Long Sentences (3)

**Direction:** Translate the following groups of sentences into English and analyze how a long or complicated sentence is formed.

1. She has a talent

   She has a talent <u>for music</u>.(介词短语做定语 后置)

   She has an <u>amazing</u> talent for music.
   (-ing 形容词,用作前置修饰语)

2. A majority voted.

   A majority voted <u>against the proposal</u>.(介词短语做定语 后置)

   An <u>overwhelming</u> majority voted against the proposal.
   (-ing 形容词,用作前置修饰语)

3. Who's the man?

   Who's the man <u>talking</u>?

   Who's the man <u>talking to your sister</u>?
   (现在分词短语做后置修饰语时的作用很像一个关系从句,主要用来叙述和句子的主要动词同时或差不多同时发生的动作。e.g., Anybody <u>touching that wire</u> will get an electric shock.)

4. Is this the book?

   Is this the book <u>recommended</u>?

   Is this the book <u>recommended by the professor</u>?
   (过去分词短语做后置修饰语通常表示其动作在句子叙述的动作之前已完成,或者没有时间性。若要叙述与主要动词同时发生的动作,要用现在分词的被动形式:He told us to keep a secret of the things <u>being discussed</u>.如果指的是未来的动作,则用不定式的被动形式:He's been invited to a meeting to be held next Monday.)

5. Most people were old friends.
   　　Most people invited were old friends.
   　　　　Most people invited to the party were old friends.
   　　　　　　（同上）
6. The bridge is in the city.
   　　The bridge is the longest in the city.
   　　　　The bridge, completed in 1994, is the longest in the city.
   　　　　　　(在书面语中,可用逗号将分词短语与句子的其他成分分开。它的作用很像一个非限制性关系从句,对所叙述的人或事物作附加说明。)

# Keys to Test One

**Tape scripts for Listening Comprehension**
**Part I Listening Comprehension**
**Section A (12 points)**

1. M: Let's go to the concert tonight.
   W: I want to, but my mother wants me to go home early first, then I can go.
   Q: Can the woman go out?

2. W: Do you sell jackets, sir?
   M: Yes, we do. They are on special sale this week. That's one for 19, two for 35.
   Q: How much does one jacket cost?

3. M: The students sang well at the concert and we all enjoyed it.
   W: It was a pity that they came second in the end.
   Q: What does the woman feel about the students' performance?

4. M: Where did you take these pictures?
   W: Last Saturday we went to Central Park. I think they turned out well, too.
   Q: What are they doing?

5. M: Have you seen Lee recently?
   W: He must be home by now. I saw him leave on his bike half an hour ago.
   Q: Where does the woman think Lee is?

6. M: May I speak to Jason Daniels please?
   W: Nobody by that name works here.
   Q: What do we learn from this conversation?

7. W: What do you think of my idea?
   M: I can't think of a better one, Julie.
   Q: What does the man think?

8. W: John, I heard you went skiing last weekend. What happened?
   M: I had a bad cold and broke my leg.
   Q: What happened to John?

9. M: If you'd like to go there for dinner this evening, I'll phone the restaurant and reserve another place.
   W: Thank you, but I promised my sister to take her to the airport.
   Q: What is the woman going to do this evening?

10. W: Does Jim play tennis?
    M: Well, that's him on the court now. He plays almost like a professional.
    Q: Where is Jim now?

11. W: Good morning, Hilton Hotel. May I help you?
    M: Hi, I'd like some information about your hotel.
    Q: What is the woman?

12. M: I'm starting training tomorrow for the basketball match.
    W: Should you be playing right away after you've just had that arm operation?
    Q: What does the woman mean?

### Section B (10 points)

Every artist knows in his heart that he is saying something to the public. Not only does he want to say it well, but he wants it to be something which has not been said before. He hopes the public will listen and understand—he wants to teach them, and he wants them to learn from him.

What visual artists like painters want to teach is easy to make out but difficult to explain, because painters translate their experiences into shapes and colors, not words. They seem to feel that a certain selection of shapes and colors, out of the countless billions possible, is exceptionally interesting for them and worth showing to us. Without their work we should never have noticed these particular shapes and colors, or have felt the delight which they brought to the artist.

Most artists take their shapes and colors from the world of nature and from human bodies in motion and repose (休息). Their choices indicate that these aspects of the world are worth looking at, that they contain beautiful sights. Contemporary artists might say that they merely choose subjects that provide an interesting pattern, that there is nothing more in it. Yet even they do not choose entirely without reference to the character of their subjects.

If one painter chooses to paint a gangrenous (生蛆的) leg and another a lake in moonlight, each of them is directing our attention to a certain aspect of the world. Each painter is telling us something, showing us something, emphasizing something—all of which means that, consciously or unconsciously, he is trying to teach us.

### Part I Listening Comprehension
### Section A (12 points)
1. C  2. A  3. D  4. C  5. C  6. B  7. C  8. C  9. D  10. A  11. D  12. B

### Section B (10 points)
1. visual   2. translate   3. shapes   4. selection

5. countless     6. exceptionally     7. worth     8. delight
9. these aspects of the world are worth looking at, that they contain beautiful sights
10. they merely choose subjects that provide an interesting pattern
11. Each painter is telling us something, showing us something, emphasizing something

**Part II Reading Comprehension (30 points)**
1-5 DBCAC     6-10 ABCBC     11-15 CDDDA     16-20 DABCC

**Part III Vocabulary & Structure (12 points)**
1-5 DABCA     6-10 CCABD     11-15 ADACA     16-20 BCAAA     21-24 DCBB

**Part IV Cloze (10 points)**
1-5 CDCAB     6-10 ABACB     11-15 CBDAD     16-20 BACDB

**Part V Translation**
**Section A (10 points)**
1. 若地址变更，请尽快在第一时间通知我们。
2. 学生在学习之余，还应有自己的兴趣爱好。
3. 她非常在意别人对她的看法。
4. 他的摄影兴趣只是一时的狂热。
5. 争论的双方似乎都下决心不打算妥协。

**Section B (10 points)**
**Direction: Translate the following sentences into English, using the words or phrases in the brackets.**
1. aspires to fame and success
2. The press had criticized her so often that
3. is the biggest barrier to
4. They take great pride in their daughter
5. were bulging with presents/gifts

**Part VI Organizing Your Ideas (6 points)**
g   f   e   d   h   b   a   c

# Never Give Up

## 🎙 Script for Lead-in Listening

Listen to the following conversation and fill in the blanks with the correct words or phrases. You may choose the words or phrases from the list given.

**John:** Hey, Wang. Do you know that my cousin has been just selected as a member of the US Olympic Gymnastics team for Athens?

**Wang:** No way! That's awesome!

**John:** Yeah. She finally made it, and she certainly deserves it. She's been taking gymnastics classes seriously since she was a little girl, like since she was only 5 or 6 years old.

**Wang:** Congratulations! She must be one of the best gymnasts in your country.

**John:** I'll say!

**Wang:** Speaking of Olympics, I've noticed that the Chinese haven't sent their best team to the World Championship this year. For example, Olympic and World champion Li Xiaopeng skipped the men's events. Do you know why?

**John:** I'm not sure.

**Wang:** It's because the Chinese Gymnastics team put their focus on the Athens Olympic Games, and only the Chinese Olympic lineup was sent to the World Championship.

**John:** I'm sure the Chinese Gymnastics team will get a few gold medals at the Olympics this time.

**Wang:** I hope so. In recent years our Chinese Gymnasts have become strong and they are getting very competitive now.

### WORDS AND EXPRESSIONS IN LEAD-IN LISTENING

**select** *v.* to choose sb/sth, esp. as being the best or most suitable
 select a card from the rack
 selected as the team leader
 Who has been selected to take part in the project?

**deserve** *v.* [not used in the continuous tenses] to be sth or have done sth for which one should receive (a reward, special treatment, etc.); to be entitled to; to merit
 The article deserves careful study.
 She deserves a reward for her efforts.
 They deserve to be sent to prison.

**take sb/sth seriously**   *v.*   to regard sb/sth as important and worth treating with respect
*You can't take her promises seriously: she never keeps her word.*
*I take this threat very seriously.*

**skip**   *v.*   not to attend (a meeting, etc.)
*skip a lecture, an appointment, a class*

**competitive**   *adj.*   of or involving competition
*competitive examinations for government posts*
*the competitive spirit*

# TEXT A

# HEART OF GOLD

## Background Information

1. **Kerri Strug**   A two-time Olympian and gold medalist. She was the youngest US Olympian at the 1992 Olympic Games in Barcelona, Spain at only 14. After four more years of hard work and training, she captured America's spirit at the 1996 Olympic Games in Atlanta. As the team competition neared its end, Kerri was up last on vault. After shocking spectators by falling and injuring her ankle on her first vault, she managed to stick the landing on her second vault before collapsing in pain, helping to secure gold for the American team. It was a moment that landed Kerri on the front page of newspapers around the world and catapulted her into the spotlight. She was only eighteen years old.

2. **Kim Zmeskal**   (born February 6, 1976 in Houston, Texas) An American retired gymnast and coach.

   *Achievement*

   First American gymnast to win four consecutive National all-around titles (Junior National Champion 1989, Senior National Champion 1990—1992)

   First and only American gymnast to win three consecutive Senior National all-around titles

   First gymnast from the United States, male or female, to become a World all-around champion

   First American gymnast to hold three World titles at once (1991 AA Champion, 1992 Beam and Floor Champion)

   First American gymnast to win world titles on both the Balance Beam and the Floor Exercise at the 1992 World Championships in Paris, France

3. **Shannon Miller**   A 7-time Olympic Medalist and 9-time World Medalist remains The Most Decorated American Gymnast, male or female, in history, having won more Olympic and

World Championship Medals than any other US gymnast.

*Major medals*

1991 Worlds: Bars silver, team silver

1992 Olympics: All-Around silver, beam silver, floor bronze, bars bronze, team bronze

1993 Worlds: All-Around gold, bars gold, floor gold

1994 Worlds: All-Around gold, beam gold

1994 Team Worlds: Team silver

1995 Worlds: Team bronze

1996 Olympics: Beam gold, team gold

4. **Bela Karolyi** (born September 13, 1942) A world-renowned Romanian gymnastics coach. He possesses Romanian and American citizenship. Together with his wife, Marta, (sometimes called Martha), Karolyi has coached both the United States and Romanian Olympic teams to medal success. He was born in Cluj, Romania.

*Awards and Accomplishments*

1972 Coaches team to a silver medal and coaches Comaneci to the individual gold, at the Eastern Bloc Friendship Cup in Sofia

1976 Brings Nadia Comaneci to the Montreal Olympics where she wins the individual gold medal; coaches Romanian team to first Olympic medals since 1960; wins Romanian Labor Union Medal

1977 Wins the Romanian national championships

1978 Wins the Friendship Cup

1979 Sweeps the European championships and the world championships

1984 Brings Mary Lou Retton to the Los Angeles Olympics where she wins the individual gold medal; coaches the United States team to first Olympic team medal since 1948

1996 Coaches the United States team to Olympic gold medal

1997 Inducted into the International Gymnastics Hall of Fame

5. **Dominique Dawes** An outstanding athlete and world-class competitor, Dominique Margaux Dawes, has broken both athletic records and racial barriers as a renowned Olympic gymnast.

Known for her spirited and explosive tumbling, "Awesome Dawesome," as she is lovingly referred to, became an international force to be reckoned with by her early teens.

*Awards*

AAUW Women of Distinction Award, 2004

"Caring Hands, Caring Hearts" Award, Ronald McDonald House Charities and Children Around the World, 2003

Inducted into USA Gymnastics Hall of Fame, 1998

Essence Award, 1997

Henry P. Iba Citizen Award, presented annually to two outstanding athletes who have demonstrated good citizenship, 1995

Sportsperson of the year by USA Gymnastics, 1994

Finalist for the AAU Sullivan Award, which recognizes the USA's top amateur athlete, 1994

## Language Points

1. **qualify**  *v.*  to have or give (sb) that qualities, training, etc. that are necessary or suitable (for sth)

    *I won't qualify until next year.*
    *A stroll round the garden hardly qualifies as exercise!*
    *The training course qualifies you to be/as a driving instructor.*

2. **final**  *n.*  last of a series of contests or competitions

    *the tennis finals*
    *the Cup Final*

3. **understatement**  *n.*  statement that expresses an idea, etc. too weakly

    *To say that he was displeased is an understatement. In fact, he was furious.*
    *To say the movie was bad is an understatement.*

4. **retire**  *v.*  to give up one's regular work, esp. because of age

    *retire on a pension at 60*
    *the retiring union leader*
    *He will retire from the army/his directorship next year.*

    **retirement**  *n.*  (instance of) retiring or being retired from work

    *go into retirement*
    *come out of retirement*

5. **leap**  *v.*  jump vigorously

    *The cat leapt from the chair.*
    *My heart leapt for joy at the news.*
    *A frog leapt out.*

6. **score**  *n.*  a. number of points, goals, etc. made by a player or team in a game, or gained in a competition, etc.

    *a high/low score*
    *What's my score?*
    *make a good score of 50 points*

    b. number of points made by both players or teams in such a game, etc.

    *keep the score*
    *The final score was 4-3.*

7. **hesitate**  *v.*  to be slow to speak or act because one feels uncertain or unwilling; pause in doubt

    *She hesitated before replying.*
    *He is still hesitating about joining/over whether to join the expedition.*
    *He hesitates at nothing.*

**hesitation** *n.* state or instance of hesitating

She agreed without the slightest hesitation.

His frequent hesitations annoyed the audience.

8. **champion** *n.* person, team, animal or plant that has defeated or excelled all others in a competition

a chess champion

a champion swimmer

The English football team were world champions in 1966.

9. **perform** *v.* a. to do (a piece of work, sth one is ordered to do, sth one has agreed to do)

perform a task/one's duty

perform an operation to save his life

b. to act (a play), play (a piece of music) or do (tricks) to entertain an audience

They are performing his play tonight.

perform skillfully on the flute

perform seals in a circus

10. **capture** *v.* a. to take (sb/sth) as a prisoner

capture an escaped convict

This advertisement will capture the attention of TV audiences.

b. to take or win (sth) by force or skill

capture a town

capture one's opponent's queen

11. **proclaim** *v.* a. to make (sth) known officially or publicly; announce

proclaim a public holiday

After its independence India was proclaimed a republic.

b. to show (sth) clearly; reveal

His accent proclaimed that he was a Scot.

12. **hide (sb/sth) from** prevent sb/sth from being known; keep secret

She tried to hide her feelings.

The future is hidden from us.

His words had a hidden meaning.

# Answer Keys

### I. Getting the Message

1. B  2. A  3. D  4. D  5. C

### II. Developing Your Vocabulary

#### Section A

1. qualified  2. retire  3. perform  4. gymnast  5. champions  6. capture

## Unit Five  Never Give Up

### Section B
1. returned to  2. referred to  3. over and over
4. come out of retirement  5. set her sights on  6. such as

## III. Recognizing Main Ideas
1. peak  2. narrowly  3. gave up  4. gymnast
5. injury  6. performed  7. competition  8. spotlight

## IV. Trying the Translation

### Section A
1. 她总是报以微笑,点一点头,却并不相信。
2. 她把两届奥运会之间的这些年看成是她一生中最糟糕的时候。
3. 能否获得团体赛冠军就看她跳的怎么样了。
4. 克里走向贝拉,告诉他她的腿没有知觉了。
5. 克里的这一跳被报纸《今日美国》赞誉为"自1980年美国曲棍球队战胜苏联队后美国队在奥运会团体比赛中的一次最伟大的胜利"。

### Section B
1. I asked where he'd been, but he didn't respond.
2. Experts referred to the discovery as a major breakthrough in medical science.
3. I don't think you are aware how much this means to me.
4. Can you explain it to me one more time?
5. The bushes hid Tom's bike completely from the passers-by.

## V. Organizing Your Ideas
b  c  f  d  a  e

## 参考译文

### 一跳辉煌

　　克里·斯特鲁格的朋友和家人不止一次地告诉她,她的时代即将到来。而她总是报以微笑,点一点头,却并不相信。这是可以理解的,因为在向职业运动生涯的最高峰冲刺的过程中,她总是与金牌擦肩而过。在那时,聚光灯总是照向像珊南·米勒、金·兹梅斯卡尔那样实力超群的体操运动员。没有成为聚光灯下的明星是因为她确实没有斐然的成绩。她还没有资格受人瞩目。在1992年奥运会的体操全能决赛中,她以0.141分的微弱差距与冠军失之交臂。这使得人们认为她在1996年的奥运会上仍将是个失败者。

　　1992年的奥运会后,她的教练贝拉·卡洛里退休了。克里只得从一个又一个队中去寻找适合她的新教练。她说那是她一生中最糟糕的时候。到了1994年事情有了转机,她的教练卡洛里复出。一年以后,离亚特兰大奥运会没几个月的时候,她在卡洛里的指导下重新投入训练,将目光瞄准了 1996 年的奥运会。

在奥运会上,媒体的目光都对准了多米尼克·达维斯、珊南·米勒等夺冠热门选手。在团体决赛的最后一天进行的最后一项比赛——跳马比赛中,克里是美国队最后一位出场的运动员。她表现的机会终于到来了。能否获得团体赛冠军就看她跳的怎么样了。在她的第一跳时,过早落地使她的脚踝严重受伤,她背上了沉重的压力。当时,她的队友和教练都认为要取得团体冠军还要看她的第二跳。他们并不知道其实她第一跳的分数已经足以为美国队赢得胜利。

克里走向她的教练贝拉,告诉他她的腿没有知觉了。贝拉告诉她必须再跳一次。"必须再跳一次吗?"克里问。贝拉也问:"你可以吗,可以吗?"她有些迟疑,"我也不知道。"然后她下定决心,说:"我可以跳,我可以,我可以。"克里知道,这是证明自己的时刻,她要向自己、队友和任何一个怀疑她实力的人证明她具备冠军的实力。而她即将获得这个冠军称号。

她带伤完成了她的第二跳,并赢得了冠军。克里的这一跳被报纸《今日美国》赞誉为"自 1980 年美国曲棍球队战胜苏联队后美国队在奥运会团体比赛中的一次最伟大的胜利"。

在颁奖仪式上,她的教练把她抱上领奖台。在国歌声中,她一条腿站立着,她的队友搀扶着她。这是历史上美国队第一次获得女子体操团体世界冠军。这也是克里第一次站在了聚光灯下。

# TEXT B

## RUN, PATTI, RUN!

## Background Information

**The Guiness Book of World Records** (known as *Guinness World Records* nowadays) A reference book published annually, containing an internationally recognized collection of world records, both human achievements and the extreme of the natural world. The book itself holds a world record, as the best-selling copyrighted series of all-time.

On 10 November 1951, Sir Hugh Beaver, then the managing director of the Guinness Brewery, went on a shooting party in North Slob, by the River Slaney in County Wexford, Ireland. He became involved in an argument: Which was the fastest game bird in Europe, the golden plover or the grouse? That evening at Castlebridge House, he realized that it was impossible to confirm in reference books whether or not the golden plover was Europe's fastest game bird.

Beaver thought that there must be numerous other questions debated nightly in the 81,400 pubs in Britain and Ireland, but there was no book with which to settle arguments about records. He realized then that a book supplying the answers to this sort of question might prove popular. Beaver's idea became reality when Guinness employee Christopher Chataway recommended student twins Norris and Ross McWhirter, who had been running a fact-finding agency in London. The brothers were commissioned to compile what became *The Guinness Book of Records* in August 1954. One thousand copies were printed and given away.

After founding the *Guinness Book of Records* at 107 Fleet Street, the first 198-page edition was bound on 27 August 1955 and went to the top of the British bestseller lists by Christmas. "It was a marketing give away—it wasn't supposed to be a money maker," said Beaver. The following year it launched in the US, and it sold 70,000 copies.

After the book became a surprise hit, many further editions were printed, eventually settling into a pattern of one revision a year, published in October to coincide with Christmas sales. The McWhirters continued to publish it and related books for many years. Both brothers had an encyclopedic memory—on the TV series *Record Breakers*, based upon the book, they would take questions posed by children in the audience on various world records, and would usually be able to give the correct answer. Ross McWhirter was assassinated by the Provisional Irish Republican Army in 1975. Following McWhirter's assassination, the feature in the show where questions about records posed by children were answered was called "Norris on the Spot".

## Language Points

1. **in view of**   taking sth into account; considering sth
    *In view of the weather, we will cancel the outing.*
    *In view of Tom's recent conduct the club has decided to suspend him until further notice.*
2. **ambitious**   *a.*   having, showing or requiring strong desire to achieve sth
    *an ambitious young manager*
    *ambitious for one's children*
    *ambitious plans to complete the project ahead of schedule*
3. **enthusiastic**   *a.*   full of strong feeling of admiration or interest
    *He doesn't know much about the subject, but he's very enthusiastic.*
    *She's very enthusiastic about singing.*
4. **inconvenience**   *n.*   a. trouble, difficulty or discomfort
    *He apologized for the inconvenience he had caused.*
    *put sb to inconvenience/suffer great inconvenience*
   b. person or thing that causes inconvenience
    *Having to change trains is a small inconvenience.*
    *put up with slight inconveniences*
5. **en route**   *(French)*   on the way
    *We stopped at Paris en route from Rome to London.*
    *They passed through Paris en route for Rome.*
6. **fracture**   *v.*   (cause sth to) break or crack
    *Her leg fractured in two places.*
    *suffer from a fractured pelvis*
    *n.*   instance of breaking (esp. a bone)
    *a fracture of the leg*
    *He had several injuries, including three fractures.*

7. **wrap**  v.  a. to cover or enclose sth (in soft or flexible material)

   I have wrapped (up) the parcels and they're ready to be posted.

   The Christmas presents were wrapped (up) in tissue paper.

   b. to wind or fold (a piece of material) round sb/sth as covering or protection

   Wrap a scarf round your neck.

   He wrapped a clean rag around his ankle.

8. **blister**  n.  a. bubble-like swelling under the skin, filled with watery liquid (caused by rubbing, burning, etc.)

   These tight shoes have given me blisters on my ankles.

   b. similar raised swelling on the surface of metal, painted wood, plants, etc.

   v.  (cause sth to) form blisters

   My feet blister easily.

   The hot sun blistered the paint.

9. **instead of sth/doing sth**   as an alternative or replacement to (sb/sth)

   Let's play cards instead of watching television.

   Instead of Graham, it was Peter who moved in.

10. **open up**   (cause sth to) begin business

    He never opens up ship on a Sunday.

    open up a new restaurant

# Answer Keys

## I. Getting the Message

### Section A

1. Y    2. N    3. N    4. NG    5. Y    6. Y

### Section B

1. ambitious...enthusiastic
2. on what she had been left
3. Run, Patti, Run
4. her lifelong dream
5. put it in a cast
6. epileptics were normal human beings with normal lives

## II. Recognizing Main Ideas

1. epileptic    2. break    3. women    4. freshman    5. run
6. Portland    7. foot    8. wrap    9. President    10. normal

**参考译文**

## 帕蒂,加油!

帕蒂·威尔森年幼时就被医生诊断出患有癫痫。她的父亲习惯每天晨跑。一天,帕蒂对父亲说:"爸爸,我真想每天跟你一起跑步,但我担心中途病情发作。"父亲回答说:"万一你病情发作,我也知道怎么处理。就让我们从现在开始跑吧!"

晨跑是她与父亲共同拥有的最快乐的时光。跑步期间,帕蒂的病一次也没发作。过了几个礼拜之后,她对父亲说:"爸爸,我真想打破女子长跑的世界纪录。"

她父亲替她查了查吉尼斯世界纪录,发现女子长跑的最高纪录是80英里。当时还在读高中一年级的帕蒂宣布:"今年我要从奥兰治县跑到旧金山(两地相距400英里)。""二年级时,要跑步到达俄勒冈州的波特兰(1500多英里);三年级的目标是圣路易斯(约2000英里);四年级要向白宫进军(3000多英里远)。"

即使身患残疾,帕蒂仍满怀理想和热情。她说癫痫只是给她带来不便的小毛病。她没有一味想着因病失去了什么,而是把全部的注意力放在仍然拥有的一切上。

中学一年级时,帕蒂身着写有"我爱癫痫病人"字样的T恤衫,一路跑到了旧金山。二年级时,班上的同学跟在她身后跑。他们制作了一副巨大的广告牌,上面写着"加油,帕蒂,加油!"(这后来成为她的座右铭)。

但在第二次前往波特兰的马拉松途中,她扭伤了一只脚的踝骨。医生告诫她必须中止跑步。

"医生,你不了解,跑步不是我一时性起,而是我终生的理想。我跑步不单是为了自己,我这样做是为了打碎束缚许多残疾人脑子的枷锁。难道没有什么方法能让我继续跑完全程吗?"医生给了她一个选择,他可以用胶布把受伤处裹起来,不用上石膏;但他警告说,"这样会非常疼,而且还会起泡。"帕蒂二话不说让医生包扎起来。帕蒂终于到达了波特兰,在俄勒冈州州长的陪同下,她跑完最后一英里。

高三那年,经过4个月连续不断的长跑,帕蒂从西海岸跑到东海岸,到达了华盛顿,并有幸与美国总统握手。她告诉总统:"我想告诉人们,癫痫患者也是正常人,也能过正常的生活。"

帕蒂的父亲说,由于帕蒂的非凡努力,他们已筹措了足够的资金,预备在全国建立19所癫痫病治疗中心。

如果帕蒂能尽她仅有的微薄之力取得如此巨大的成就,那么身心健全的我们难道不应该超越自我,有更大的作为吗?

# Reading in Focus

分词表示的逻辑关系 Sentences with Participles

Direction: You are asked to read the following sentences and identify the relationship between the adverbials and the main clauses. Then specify the types of participle phrases used in these sentences and the relationship between these phrases and the subjects of the main clauses. Write your answer in Chinese in the blanks and brackets respectively.

1. 说明主句动作发生的原因　（现在分词，主动的主谓关系）
2. 说明主句动作发生的时间　（现在分词，主动的主谓关系）
3. 说明主句动作发生的时间　（现在分词，主动的主谓关系）
4. 说明主句动作发生的伴随状态　（过去分词，被动的主谓关系）
5. 说明主句动作发生的原因　（过去分词，被动的主谓关系）
6. 说明主句动作发生的背景，与主句形成转折关系　（现在分词，主动的主谓关系）
7. 说明主句动作发生的条件　（过去分词，被动的主谓关系）
8. 说明主句动作发生的伴随状态　（现在分词，主动的主谓关系）
9. 说明主句动作发生的条件　（现在分词，主动的主谓关系）
10. 说明主句动作发生的结果　（现在分词，主动的主谓关系）

# City Symbol

## Script for Lead-in Listening

Listen to the following interview and fill in the blanks with the correct words or phrases. You may choose the words or phrases from the list given.

**Ann:** Excuse me, could you tell me the way to the library at the Statue of Liberty National Monument?

**Gary:** Go straight, then turn left and you'll find a tall building. The library is on the third floor, in the west wing of the Ellis Island Immigration Museum.

**Ann:** Thanks a lot.

**Gary:** You're welcome.

**Ann:** But I want to know what kind of library it is. Is it different from other libraries?

**Gary:** It's a research library with subject emphasis on the Statue of Liberty, Ellis Island, immigration, and ethnic groups.

**Ann:** Oh, I see. Apart from books, are there any photographs of the Statue of Liberty and Ellis Island in the library?

**Gary:** Of course. There are historic photographs of the Statue of Liberty and Ellis Island including unique photograph collections by Augustus F. Sherman, and Colonel John B. Weber; the Foxlee Papers, the Maud Mosher Papers, and a sixteen volume collection of periodicals and newspaper articles by Gino Speranza on immigration and related subjects between 1900 and 1927.

**Ann:** Great! Can I borrow books and photographs freely?

**Gary:** I'm afraid you can't. Library materials include books, manuscripts, films, photographs and general reference files which may only be used by researchers on site. Call (212) 363-3200, ext. 158 or 161 or fax (212) 363-6302 for further information.

**Ann:** That's kind of you. Thank you very much.

### WORDS AND EXPRESSIONS IN LEAD-IN LISTENING

**wing**  *n.*  part of a building that projects from the main part.
  *They built a new wing of a hospital last year.*

**research**  *n.*  careful study or investigation, esp in order to discover new facts or information
  *He is doing research in ancient history.*

**emphasis on sth**  (placing of)  special meaning, value or importance (of sth)
   *Some schools place great emphasis on language study.*

**immigration**  *n.*  (instance of) moving of people from one country to come to live in anoter country permanently

**ethnic**  *a.*  of a national, racial or tribal group that has a common cultural tradition

**unique**  *a.*  being the only one of its type
   *The painting is a unique work of art.*

**periodical**  *n.*  (magazine or other publication) that is published at regular intervals, eg weekly or monthly

**I'm afraid (that...)**  (usually without that) to express politely a piece of information that may be unwelcome
   *I'm afraid we can't come.*
   *I can't help I'm afraid.*

**manuscript**  *n.*  thing written by hand, not typed or printed

# TEXT A

# THE STATUE OF LIBERTY—A DIPLOMATIC GIFT

 **Background Information**

**1. Liberty Enlightening the World**  (French: La liberté éclairant le monde) Known more commonly as the Statue of Liberty (Statue de la Liberté), is a large statue that was presented to the United States by the people of France in 1886. It stands at Liberty Island (part of New York but physically on the New Jersey side of the New York Harbor) as a welcome to all visitors, immigrants, and returning Americans. The copper patina-clad statue, dedicated on October 28, 1886, commemorates the centennial of the United States and is a gesture of friendship from France to the US Frédéric Auguste Bartholdi sculpted the statue and obtained a US patent useful for raising construction funds through the sale of miniatures. Alexandre Gustave Eiffel (designer of the Eiffel Tower) engineered the internal structure.

The statue is 151 feet (46.02 m) tall, but with the pedestal and foundation, it is 305 feet (92.96 m) tall. Worldwide, the Statue of Liberty is one of the most recognizable icons of the United States, and, more generally, represents liberty and escape from oppression. The Statue of Liberty was, from 1886 until the jet age, often one of the first glimpses of the United States for millions of immigrants after ocean voyages from Europe. Visually, the Statue of Liberty appears to draw inspiration from il Sancarlone or the Colossus of Rhodes. The statue is a central part of Statue of Liberty National Monument, administered by the National Park Service.

**2. Benjamin Franklin** (January 17, 1706 [O.S. January 6, 1706]—April 17, 1790) One of the Founding Fathers of the United States of America. A noted polymath, Franklin was a leading author and printer, satirist, political theorist, politician, scientist, inventor, civic activist, statesman and diplomat. As a scientist he was a major figure in the Enlightenment and the history of physics for his discoveries and theories regarding electricity. He invented the lightning rod, bifocals, the Franklin stove, a carriage odometer, and a musical instrument. He formed both the first public lending library in America and first fire department in Pennsylvania. He was an early proponent of colonial unity and as a political writer and activist he, more than anyone, invented the idea of an American nation and as a diplomat during the American Revolution, he secured the French alliance that helped to make independence possible.

He played a major role in establishing the University of Pennsylvania and Franklin & Marshall College and was elected the first president of the American Philosophical Society. Franklin became a national hero in America when he spearheaded the effort to have Parliament repeal the unpopular Stamp Act. An accomplished diplomat, he was widely admired among the French as American minister to Paris and was a major figure in the development of positive Franco-American relations. From 1775 to 1776, Franklin was Postmaster General under the Continental Congress and from 1785 to 1788 was President of the Supreme Executive Council of Pennsylvania. Toward the end of his life, he became one of the most prominent abolitionists.

Franklin's colorful life and legacy of scientific and political achievement, and status as one of America's most influential Founding Fathers, has seen Franklin honored on coinage and money; warships; the names of many towns, counties, educational institutions, namesakes, and companies; and more than two centuries after his death, countless cultural references.

**3. A National Monument** In the United States it is a protected area that is similar to a national park (specifically a US National Park) except that the President of the United States can quickly declare an area of the United States to be a national monument without Congressional approval. National monuments receive less funding and afford fewer protections to wildlife than national parks.

National monuments are managed by the National Park Service, USDA Forest Service, United States Fish and Wildlife Service or by the Bureau of Land Management.

**4. Édouard René Lefèvre de Laboulaye** (January 18, 1811 in Paris—May 25, 1883 in Paris) A French jurist. Laboulaye was received at the bar in 1842, and was chosen professor of comparative law at the Collège de France in 1849. Following the Paris Commune of 1870, he was elected to the national assembly, representing the département of the Seine. As secretary of the committee of thirty on the constitution he was effective in combatting the Monarchists in establishing the Third Republic. In 1875 he was elected a life senator, and in 1876 he was appointed administrator of the Collège de France, resuming his lectures on comparative legislation in 1877. Laboulaye was also chairman of the French Anti-Slavery Society.

Nevertheless, he is most remembered as the intellectual creator of the Statue of Liberty.

5. **Joseph Pulitzer** (April 10, 1847—October 29, 1911) A Hungarian-American publisher best known for posthumously establishing the Pulitzer Prizes and (along with William Randolph Hearst) for originating yellow journalism.

6. **Frédéric Auguste Bartholdi** (August 2, 1834—October 4, 1904) A French sculptor. He is also known as Amilcar Hasenfratz.

His first masterpiece is General Rapp's monument in Colmar. Then he had a lot of success in Alsace.

The work for which he is most famous is the Statue of Liberty, donated in 1886 by the Union Franco-Americaine (Franco-American Union), founded by Edouard de Laboulaye, to the United States. It was rumored all over France that the face of the Statue of Liberty was modeled after Bartholdi's mother; and the body after his mistress. Before starting his commission, Bartholdi traveled to the United States to personally select New York Harbor as the site for the statue.

In 1879, Bartholdi was awarded design patent US Patent D11,023 for the Statue of Liberty. This patent covered the sale of small copies of the statue. Proceeds from the sale of the statues helped raise money to build the full statue.

Bartholdi would go on to become one of the most celebrated of the 19th century sculptors, famous both in Europe and in North America.

7. **Alexandre Gustave Eiffel** (December 15, 1832—December 27, 1923) A French structural engineer and architect and a specialist of metallic structures. He is famous for designing the Eiffel Tower, built 1887—1889 for the 1889 Universal Exposition in Paris, France, the Basilica Minore de San Sebastian, the only all-steel basilica in Asia, and the armature for the Statue of Liberty, New York Harbor, US.

8. **President Grover Cleveland** (March 18, 1837—June 24, 1908) The twenty-second and twenty-fourth President of the United States. Cleveland is the only President to serve two non-consecutive terms (1885—1889 and 1893—1897). He was the winner of the popular vote for President three times—in 1884, 1888, and 1892—and was the only Democrat elected to the Presidency in the era of Republican political domination that lasted from 1860 to 1912. Cleveland's admirers praise him for his honesty, independence, integrity, and commitment to the principles of classical liberalism. As a leader of the Bourbon Democrats, he opposed imperialism, taxes, subsidies and inflationary policies, but as a reformer he also worked against corruption, patronage, and bossism.

9. **Ellis Island** A symbol of America's immigrant heritage. From 1892 to 1954, this immigrant depot processed the greatest tide of incoming humanity in the nations history. Nearly twelve million landed here in their search of freedom of speech and religion, and for economic opportunity.

10. **President Ronald Reagan** (February 6, 1911—June 5, 2004) The 40th President of the United States (1981—1989) and the 33rd Governor of California (1967—1975). Born in Illinois, Reagan moved to Los Angeles, California in the 1930s, where he became an actor,

president of the Screen Actors Guild (SAG), and a spokesman for General Electric (GE). His start in politics occurred during his work for GE; originally a member of the Democratic Party, he switched to the Republican Party in 1962. After delivering a rousing speech in support of Barry Goldwater's presidential candidacy in 1964, he was persuaded to seek the California governorship, winning two years later and again in 1970. He was defeated in his run for the Republican presidential nomination in 1968 as well as 1976, but won both the nomination and election in 1980.

## Language Points

1. **recognition**  *n.*  recognizing or being recognized

    *He has won wide recognition in the field of tropical medicine.*

    *The town has altered out of all recognition since I was last here.*

    *Britain's recognition of establishment of diplomatic relations with the new regime is unlikely.*

2. **cultivate**  *v.*  (try to) acquire or develop (a relationship, an attitude, etc.)

    *You must cultivate people who can help you in business.*

    *He wants to cultivate new friends.*

3. **negotiation**  *n.*  discussion aimed at reaching an agreement; negotiating

    *The price is a matter of/for negotiation.*

    *Negotiation of the sale took a long time.*

    *A settlement was reached after lengthy negotiations.*

4. **commitment**  *n.*  thing one has promised to do; state of being dedicated or devoted (to sth)

    *They held us to our commitment.*

    *They are allowed flexible hours to meet family commitments.*

    *I'm overworked at the moment—I've taken on too many commitments.*

    *We're looking for someone with a real sense of commitment to the job.*

5. **sculptor**  *n.*  person who makes sculpture

    *Michelangelo was a well-known sculptor, famous for his masterpiece David.*

    *The statue was created by a French sculptor.*

6. **dedicate**  *v.*  to give completely (your energy, time, etc.)

    *He has dedicated his life to scientific research.*

    *The new President said she would dedicate herself to protecting the rights of the old, the sick and the homeless.*

    **dedicated**  *adj.*  working hard at sth because it is important

    *She's completely dedicated to her work.*

    *The Green Party is dedicated to protecting the environment.*

    *He's a wonderful doctor-he's very dedicated (= works very hard).*

    **be dedicated to**  to give a lot of your time and effort to a particular activity or purpose because you think it important

*She is dedicated to her job.*
*Her life is dedicated to helping the poor.*

7. **deteriorate**   *v.*   to become worse in quality or condition
    *Relations between the two countries began to deteriorate in 1965.*
    *His work has deteriorated in recent years.*
    *His health deteriorated with age.*

8. **designate**   *v.*   to give a particular name, title or position to sb
    *The two parts of the diagram were designated A and B.*
    *Smith was designated chairman.*
    *The chairman has designated Christina as his successor.*

9. **centennial**   *n.*   100th anniversary of sth
    *They are going to hold a party to celebrate the centennial of the university.*
    *The club will celebrate its centennial next year.*

10. **huddle**   *v.*   (cause sb/sth to) crowd or be heaped together, esp. in a small space
    *We all huddled around the radio to hear the news.*
    *Nearly a half of all the industrial workers of China huddled in Shanghai.*
    *The clothes lay huddled up in a pile in the corner.*

11. **yearning**   *v.*   (for sb/sth) to desire strongly or with compassion or tenderness, be filled with longing
    *He yearned for his home and family.*
    *She yearned to return to her native country.*
    *We yearn for beauty, truth and meaning in our lives.*

12. **wretched**   *a.*   very unhappy
    *The wretched man has lost all his money.*
    *These children are the wretched survivors of the earth.*
    *His stomachache made him feel wretched all day.*

 # Answer Keys

## I. Getting the Message
1. C   2. B   3. C   4. A   5. B

## II. Developing Your Vocabulary

### Section A
1. dedicated   2. commitment   3. huddled   4. raise   5. shipped   6. attraction

### Section B
1. as a result of   2. dedicated to   3. on behalf of
4. gave no sign   5. broke into   6. present... to

## III. Recognizing Main Ideas

1. designed　　2. international　　3. throughout　　4. symbol
5. escapes from　6. until　　　　　7. one of　　　　8. voyages

## IV. Trying the Translation

### Section A

1. 对成千上万的移民来说,自由女神像表达着美国人民向往自由,争取民主,渴望外交的理想。
2. 在巴黎居住的那段时间,作为美国大使,他就和法国政府和法国人民培养了感情。
3. 于是,法国士兵也加入了驱赶美国殖民者的战争队伍中。
4. 1886年10月28日,格罗弗·克利夫兰总统代表美国人民接过了这个雕塑。
5. 到达美洲之后过了将近一个世纪,自由女神像就开始有破损了。

### Section B

1. She was designated (as) sportswoman of the year.
2. He is dedicated to his favourite teaching job.
3. The price is a matter of/for negotiation.
4. These cars were shipped from France last week.
5. On behalf of all the staffs and myself I thank you for your help.

## V. Organizing Your Ideas

b　d　f　a　c　e

## 参考译文

### 自由女神像——外交礼物

　　美国收到的最高的礼物是什么?是坐落于纽约港的自由女神像。她,高152英尺,是100多年前法国人民送给美国人民的纪念物,象征着美法两国人民的友谊。对成千上万的移民来说,自由女神像表达着美国人民向往自由,争取民主,渴望外交的理想。

　　1776年,美国要求从大英帝国获取自由的那一年,美法两国之间就开始建立关系。革命战争时期,本杰明·弗兰克林和许多人一样就活跃在外交领域的前沿;在巴黎居住的那段时间,作为美国大使,他就和法国政府和法国人民培养了感情。于是,法国士兵也加入了驱赶美国殖民者的战争队伍中。在战争结束的时候,美国和大英帝国在巴黎进行了和平谈判。

　　1865年,法国的爱德华·德·拉布莱伊产生了设计一个巨大雕塑的念头,以此来纪念美法两国的友谊以及他们为了和平而作出的努力。为了筹措资金,他组建了美法联盟。约瑟夫·普利策则通过在他的报纸上开辟专栏进行宣传来获取美国民众的帮助。法国雕刻家奥古斯特·巴托尔迪和建筑工程师埃菲尔在巴黎完成了这项建造工程。1884年7月4日,自由女神像正式赠给美国。整个塑像被分成350个独立的碎片,装在214个集装箱,横穿大西洋,航运到达美国。1886年10月28日,格罗弗·克利夫兰总统代表美国人民接过了这个雕塑。

爱丽斯岛,欧洲移民到达美洲大陆的第一站,是"自由女神铜像国家纪念碑"的一部分。1892年到1924年,两千两百多万的欧洲乘客在经过爱丽斯岛和纽约港的时候可以看到这座雕像。1924年,这个标志着自由的雕塑被列为国家文物,在20世纪作为美国一个主要景点吸引了众多游客。

到达美洲之后过了将近一个世纪,自由女神像就开始有破损了。20世纪80年代初期,罗纳德·里根总统为了恢复她原始的美丽就组建了爱丽斯岛自由雕塑委员会。这一修复需要两亿三千多万。1984年,在雕像修复伊始,联合国就将该雕像列为世界文化遗产。1986年7月4号,在她落成仪式的百年纪念日,新修复过的女神像在自由周期间再次展现在了公众面前。

自由女神像的底座铭刻有女诗人爱玛·拉扎露丝的诗:

> 把你,
> 那劳瘁贫贱的流民
> 那向往自由呼吸,
> 又被无情抛弃
> 那拥挤于彼岸悲惨哀吟
> 那骤雨暴风中翻覆的惊魂
> 全都给我!
> 我高举灯盏伫立金门!

## THE MANNEKEN PIS

### Background Information

1. **Copenhagen**  The capital of Denmark. It is situated on the Zealand and Amager Islands and is separated from Malmo, Sweden by the Oresund. With the completion of the transnational Oresund Bridge in 2000, Copenhagen and the Swedish city of Malmo are connected by a car/rail link and are in the process of integrating their labour markets, resulting in the number of commuters from both sides growing annually. In 2007, the magazine *Monocle* listed Copenhagen second in their Top 20 Most Livable Cities Chart. In addition, it has also been classified as a GaWC Cultural World City, while it is 3rd in Western Europe in the rivalry over regional headquarters and distribution centres, only surpassed by London and Paris. The original designation for the city, from which the contemporary Danish name is derived, was Køpmannæhafn, "merchants' harbour". The English name for the city is derived from its Low German name, Kopenhagen. The element hafnium is named after the city's Latin name, Hafnia.

2. **Brussels**  The capital and largest city of Belgium, and the administrative heart of the European

Union. Brussels has grown from a 10th century fortress town founded by Charlemagne's grandson into a city of over one million inhabitants. Brussels is also capital of the Brussels-Capital Region, of Flanders and of the French Community of Belgium. It is not, however, the capital of the Walloon Region (Wallonia), whose capital is Namur. Depending on the context, the word Brussels may mean the largest municipality of the Brussels-Capital Region officially called the City of Brussels (ca. 140,000 inhabitants), the Brussels-Capital Region (1,067,162 inhabitants as of 1 February 2008) or, the metropolitan area of Brussels (from 2,100,000 to more or less 2,700,000 inhabitants). Brussels is considered the de facto capital of the European Union (EU), and hosts many of its key institutions. NATO, the Western European Union and EUROCONTROL are also headquartered in the city.

3. **Manneken Pis** (Dutch for little man pee)   A Brussels landmark. It is a small bronze fountain sculpture depicting a naked little boy urinating into the fountain's basin. On many occasions the statue is dressed in a costume. His wardrobe now consists of several hundred different costumes. The costumes are changed according to a schedule managed by the non-profit association The Friends of Manneken-Pis, in ceremonies that are often accompanied by brass band music. Since 1987, the Manneken has had a female equivalent, Jeanneke Pis.

4. **Belgium**   A country in northwest Europe. It is a founding member of the European Union and hosts its headquarters, as well as those of other major international organizations, including NATO. Belgium covers an area of 30,528 square kilometers (11,787 square miles) and has a population of about 10.5 million.

5. **Jérôme Duquesnoy** (1602—1654)   One of the most renowned sculptors of the seventeenth century, but for decades after his death he was better known for his conviction and execution on charges of sodomysodomy than for his impish yet polished style of sculpture.

   Born into a Brussels family of artists at the beginning of the seventeenth century, Jérôme Duquesnoy lived his first twenty years in the shadow of his famous father, Jérôme Duquesnoy the Elder (who re-cast the famous Mannekin Pis [1619], the urinating boy that still stands as Brussels' signature fountain) and his brother François, who showed artistic promise at an early age.

6. **Geraardsbergen** (French: Grammont)   A city and municipality located in the Belgian province of East Flanders. On January 1st, 2006 Geraardsbergen had a total population of 31,380. The total area is 79.71 km$^2$ which gives a population density of 394 inhabitants per km$^2$.

7. **Flanders** (Dutch: Vlaanderen)   It has historically been a region overlapping parts of modern Belgium, France, and the Netherlands. Today, Flanders designates either the Flemish Community, which includes Flemish-speaking residents of the Brussels-Capital Region, or the Flemish Region, which does not. The parliament and government govern both the Community and the Region, even though they are not co-extensive.

   West Flanders and East Flanders are two of the five provinces of the Flemish Region, both located in its western part. French Flanders may designate the departement called Nord (North) or the larger Nord-Pas de Calais region in which Nord is located. Zeelandic Flanders, in Dutch Zeeuws-Vlaanderen, refers to a part of the Netherlands located in Zeeland.

**8. Elvis Presley** (January 8, 1935—August 16, 1977)  An American singer, musician and actor. He is a cultural icon, often known as "The King of Rock & Roll", or simply "The King".

Presley began his career as one of the first performers of rockabilly, an uptempo fusion of country and rhythm and blues with a strong back beat.  His novel versions of existing songs, mixing "black" and "white" sounds, made him popular—and controversial—as did his uninhibited stage and television performances. He recorded songs in the rock and roll genre, with tracks like "Hound Dog" and "Jailhouse Rock" later embodying the style. Presley had a versatile voice and had unusually wide success encompassing other genres,  including gospel, blues, ballads and pop. To date, he has been inducted into four music halls of fame.

In the 1960s,  Presley made the majority of his thirty-three movies—mainly poorly reviewed musicals. In 1968, he returned to live music in a television special and thereafter performed across the US, notably in Las Vegas. Throughout his career, he set records for concert attendance, television ratings and recordings sales. He is one of the best-selling and most influential artists in the history of popular music.  Health problems plagued Presley in later life which,  coupled with a punishing tour schedule and addiction to prescription medication,  led to his premature death at age 42.

**9. Mickey Mouse**  Walt Disney's most famous character, made his screen debut on November 18, 1928, as star of the first sound cartoon, Steamboat Willie. Since his debut, Mickey Mouse has become an international personality whose success laid the financial foundation upon which Walt Disney built his creative organization. Besides being the personification of everything Disney,  Mickey Mouse has become one of the most universal symbols of the Twentieth Century.

Mickey Mouse was born in Walt Disney's imagination early in 1928 on a train ride from New York to Los Angeles. Walt was returning with his wife from a business meeting at which his cartoon creation, Oswald the Rabbit, had been wrestled from him by his financial backers. Only 26 at the time and with an active cartoon studio in Hollywood, Walt had gone east to arrange for a new contract and more money to improve the quality of his Oswald pictures.  The moneymen declined,  and since the character was copyrighted under their name,  they took control of it. "... So I was all alone and had nothing," Walt recalled later. "Mrs. Disney and I were coming back from New York on the train and I had to have something I could tell them. I've lost Oswald so,  I had this mouse in the back of my head because a mouse is sort of a sympathetic character in spite of the fact that everybody's frightened of a mouse including myself" Walt spent the return train ride conjuring up a little mouse in red velvet pants and named him  "Mortimer,"  but by the time the train screeched into the terminal station in Los Angeles, the new dream mouse had been rechristened. Walt's wife, Lillian, thought the name "Mortimer" was too pompous and suggested "Mickey." A star was born!

## Language Points

1. **compromise**  *v.*  to settle a dispute, etc. by making a compromise

    *I wanted to go to Greece, and my wife wanted to go to Spain, so we compromised on it.*
    *Finally they compromised over the hard-fought text.*

2. **flood**  *v.*  (cause a place that is usually dry to) be filled or overflow with water

    *The cellar floods whenever it rains heavily.*
    *The river had burst its banks and flooded the valley.*

3. **trace**  *v.*  to find the origin of sth

    *He traces his descent back to an old Norman family.*
    *Her fear of water can be traced back to a childhood accident.*
    *The cause of the fire was traced to a faulty fuse-box.*

4. **wither**  *v.*  to become dry, shrivelled or dead

    *The flowers will wither if you don't put them in water.*
    *Their hopes gradually withered away.*

5. **plunder**  *v.*  to steal (goods) from a place, esp during a time of war or civil disorder

    *The conquerors advanced, killing and plundering as they went.*
    *The invaders plundered food and valuables from coastal towns and villages.*

6. **pee**  *v.*  (informal) to urinate

    *The little boy is peeing against a tree.*
    *Don't let kids pee everywhere in the park.*

7. **wardrobe**  *n.*  place where clothes are stored, usu. a large cupboard with shelves and a rail for hanging things on

    *She asked her husband to buy her a new wardrobe for her more clothes.*
    *Would you like another wardrobe for more new clothes?*

8. **costume**  *n. [C, U]*  garment or style of dress, esp. of a particular period or group or for a particular activity

    *We're going to the party in eighteenth-century costume.*
    *He likes the traditional costume of the peasants.*

9. **gear**  *n.*  equipment, clothing, etc.

    *All his camping gear was packed in the rucksack.*
    *We're only going for two days; you don't need to bring so much gear.*
    *The girl is wearing her party gear.*

10. **folklorist**  *n.*  person who studies folklore, esp. as an academic subject

    *The old man is a well-known folklorist in the world.*
    *Do you know any folklorists in the county?*

11. **attach**  *v.*  to fasten or join sth (to sth)

    *The abalone attacked itself to rocks.*
    *A proviso attaches to the contract.*

12. **outfit**   *n.*   set of clothes worn together (esp. for a particular occasion or purpose)

   She bought a new outfit for her daughter's wedding.

   The tennis player is wearing a white tennis outfit.

13. **witch**   *n.*   woman thought to have evil magic power

   You can't believe what the witch has just told you.

   I would not what the witch has said just now.

14. **spot**   *v.*   to pick out (one person or thing from many); catch sight of; recognize

   He finally spotted just the shirt he wanted.

   I can't spot the difference between them.

   He was spotted by police boarding a plane for Paris.

15. **token**   *n.*   sign, symbol or evidence of sth

   A white flag is used as a token of surrender.

   These flowers are a small token of my gratitude.

   His actions are a token of his sincerity.

# Answer Keys

## I. Getting the Message

### Section A
1. N    2. N    3. N    4. N    5. NG    6. Y

### Section B
1. big as the Statue of Liberty
2. a new bronze statue to replace
3. different people from different countries.
4. into a statue by a witch.
5. has been stolen several times by different kinds of people
6. it is not often dressed

## II. Recognizing Main Ideas

1. landmark      2. bronze      3. sculpture      4. boy           5. basin
6. occasions     7. dressed     8. according to   9. non-profit   10. female

## 小尿童

纽约有自由女神像,哥本哈根有美人鱼,布鲁塞尔有小尿童。这尊雕像几世纪以来一直是该城市一道亮丽的风景线。大多数人看到这个小家伙的第一反应就是无比的惊叹:"看啊,他是多么的娇小啊!为什么每个人都想来看看他呢?"然而布鲁塞尔的人们却接受了他的一切——小巧玲珑。假设他和自由女神像一样大,那么布鲁塞尔就会人满为患。

事实上,没有人知道"小尿童"立在那儿的原因。人们认为他仅仅是为中世纪人们提供淡水的喷泉的一个点缀。15世纪,一个名为"小尿童"的喷泉就出现在斯都夫街/恒温街了。官方记载可以追溯到1619年8月13日。当时全市人民要求雕刻家杰罗姆·杜克恩诺雕刻一个新的青铜"小尿童"去替换那个旧的衰残的雕像。在历史的进程中,这个小雕像总是被保存起来以免遭到侵略者的毁坏。这个"小尿童"曾多次被侵略兵偷走,甚至位于佛兰德斯的赫拉尔兹贝亨小镇的市民都想把他据为己有,他们宣称要拥有比利时最古老的"尿童雕像"。

许多人都不知道这个"小尿童"经常盛装出现。他一度曾有个衣橱,里面有600多件服装,这些服装都保存在国王大厦,或位于布鲁塞尔市中心的大广场的市博物馆里。1698年5月1日,奥属尼兰德人统治者在布鲁塞尔行会组织的一次节日盛会上送给他第一套服装。接着,更多的服装接踵而来。甚至现在民俗学者在参观布鲁塞尔时,都会有衣服送给他。为了回报这些送礼物的人,"小尿童"就给他们提供现成的装在雕像上桶里的啤酒。这些服装中有一些比较特殊,如:猫王埃尔维斯·普雷斯利的全套服装,和一套米老鼠服装。

关于"小尿童"有很多传说。有一则是这样子的:一个小男孩尿湿了巫婆的门,那个巫婆就住在现如今喷泉所在地。巫婆很生气,就把小男孩变成了一尊雕像。

还有另外一则:一名男子丢了他的小儿子,两天之后,他在现在的喷泉所在地附近找到了他,当时孩子正在撒尿。出于感激,那个父亲就为喷泉建造了一个撒尿小男孩雕像。

## Reading in Focus

连词——意义承接的纽带 Connections between Sentences

I. **Direction: Choose the best answer to complete the following sentences.**

1. A　　2. B　　3. B　　4. D　　5. B

**II. Direction: Fill in the blanks, using proper conjunctions.**

1. but  2. nor  3. so that (in order that)  4. what/whatever  5. though
6. while  7. and  8. even if  9. or  10. for

**III. Direction: Read the following paragraph carefully, and then pick out all the conjunctions in it. (omitted)**

# Unit Seven

## Ultimate Challenge

 ### Script for Lead-in Listening

Listen to the following conversation and fill in the blanks with the correct words or phrases. You may choose the words or phrases from the list given.

Tom: Are extreme sports popular in your country?
Barbara: They're not very popular. Only a small number of people actually do them. Although many people enjoy watching them on TV. There's a very popular TV program each week, which is about extreme sports and the people who participate in them.
Tom: Which sports are usually featured in the program?
Barbara: Bungee jumping, skydiving, and cliff diving are the most common, but there are others, such as motor racing and skateboarding.
Tom: I think that the people who do skateboarding are very skilled. It must take a lot of practice to stay on the skateboard while doing so many jumps and turns.
Barbara: The kids who do it are so young. Well, it's better for them than sitting at home watching TV all day!

### WORDS AND PHRASES IN LEAD-IN LISTENING

**feature** *v.* to give a prominent part to sb/sth
*a film that features a new French actress*

**feature in sth** to have an important prominent part in sth
*Does a new job feature in your future plans?*
*A study of language should feature in an English literature course.*

**skydiving** *n.* the sport of jumping from a plane and falling through the sky before opening a parachute

**cliff** *n.* a large area of rock or a mountain with a very steep side, often at the edge of the sea or a river

**skilled** *adj.* someone who is skilled has the training and experience that is needed to do something well
*Skilled craftsmen, such as carpenters, are in great demand.*
*The company is fortunate to have such highly skilled workers.*

**skilled at/in**
*She's very skilled at dealing with the public.*

The school offers a program for students who are skilled in metalwork.

**participate in**   to take part in an activity or event

Everyone in the class is expected to participate actively in these discussions.

They welcomed the opportunity to participate fully in the life of the village.

# BUNGEE JUMPING

## Background Information

1. **Vanuatu**   A country in the southwest Pacific Ocean, East of Australia, made up of a chain of volcanic islands. Population: 192,190 (2001). Capital: Vila. Vanuatu was formerly called the New Hebrides, and it is an independent member of the British commonwealth.

2. **April Fools' Day**   April 1st is a day when people traditionally like to try to make a fool of someone else and laugh at them. It is a day to be careful, or you could easily get tricked by someone.

   What kind of jokes do people play on April Fool's Day?   There are lots of simple tricks that you can play on your friends.   For example, you could wear a black sweater and pull a piece of white thread through it, so that people try to pull it off. You could change the time on someone's alarm clock so that they're late for work.   Or glue a coin to the floor and see how many people try to pick it up.

   All these are small-scale practical jokes which you might play on one other person or a few people.   But there's also a tradition of large companies attempting to fool a lot of people. The media often try to make people believe something which is not true.   Newspapers publish some ludicrous stories every year, although some of them are actually true. It's entertaining to try to guess which stories are true and which are fake. In the April Fool's stories, they often include a clue to the fact that it's a joke.   Radio and television programs have also fooled many people by broadcasting reports which are untrue.   One program announced the invention of an amazing new weight-loss product—water which contained minus calories!

   And one of the most famous hoaxes ever was broadcast by the BBC itself in 1957! A very serious news program called Panorama reported on the poor spaghetti harvest in Switzerland, and showed pictures of farmers picking spaghetti from trees! Hundreds of people were taken in and wrote to the BBC asking how to grow their own spaghetti.

3. **Oxford Dangerous Sports Club**   Formed in the seventies, the group's original members consisted of David Kirke, Chris Baker, Ed Hulton, and Alan Weston. These dare devils were an unlikely mix of art and engineering students. From 1979 to 1989, they wreaked havoc in the UK and in other corners of the world.

On April Fools' Day, 1979, the DSC's first public stunt was a bungee jump off the Clifton Suspension Bridge in Bristol, England. This was, in fact, the very first bungee jump in history. Then engineering student David Kirke has been credited with engineering the elastic chord used for this first jump.

For their next stunt, the DSC flew to San Francisco where members bungee jumped off the Golden Gate Bridge.

This gained them enough notoriety to attract producers from the American television reality series, "That's Incredible." For the benefit of the TV cameras, DSC members bungee jumped off Colorado's Royal Gorge Suspension Bridge. It was this televised event that launched bungee jumping as the first popular extreme sport.

4. **New Zealand**  A country consisting of two main islands, the North Island and the South Island, and several smaller ones, in the Pacific Ocean southeast of Australia. Population: 3,864,000 (2001). Capital: Wellington. Farming, especially sheep farming, is important to the New Zealand economy. About 10% of the population are Maori people, who first came to New Zealand around the 9th century AD. Most of the rest of the population are people who came from the UK in the 19th and 20th centuries.

5. **Alan John Hackett**  Born in Auckland in May 1958, and grew up in the sun and surf of the North Shore. AJ Hackett, as his mother might call him, is one man who is seriously adventuresome. Into building, climbing and bungee jumping, you could see him as a mother's nightmare.

His love for adventure has later on turned into a very lucrative career. The demand for the addictive thrill of bungee jumping has led to the development of 10 bungee sites around the world including a purpose built double suspension jump platform of a disused railway viaduct in Normandy, France.

Starting his own adventures with rubber (rather than vine), and heights during the mid 1980's AJ says he's not as mad, as some may think, but enjoys the challenge of a calculated risk. With a group of fellow adrenaline junkies AJ progressively jumped higher and higher, utilizing the services of university students to research the rubber and technicalities of the equipment. He says the business started when a group of people who bungee jumped with him grew out of proportion. Between 1986 and 1988, AJ bungee jumped in a variety of places and off prominent landmarks all around the world, including the Eiffel Tower.

Meeting his wife while staying in France, Caroline became part of the team that helped AJ jump off the Eiffel Tower. AJ says the jump from the Eiffel Tower was perfect. He says they avoided security by covering the cameras with umbrellas or cardboard while two of the team distracted the guards. Setting up camp late at night the team stayed in the tower until first light when AJ bungee jumped down to be arrested (while drinking champagne) by some very confused policemen.

After the Eiffel Tower jump in 1987, AJ and team attempted the Statue of Liberty but were unfortunately caught before completing the task. He says this brought an end to the illegal side of his bungee jumping career and in late 1988, he set up his first commercial bungee site in Queenstown, New Zealand. Now a dad of three and a permanent resident of France, AJ travels around his bungee sites regularly and is in Cairns every three months. AJ considers his Cairns site as his home and is often found working on the site, jumping and talking to customers. The tower is the first purpose built site in the world and has celebrated its 15 years of thrilling people silly. As with all of AJ's sites, there is always something unique, and at this site, customers have the choice of 15 different jump styles and even a roof jump option for the extreme enthusiasts. The visionary AJ once said. "Everyday you should remind yourself that you're still alive". That's a mantra worth living for.

Today AJ Hackett International is a truly global organization, with operations in Australia, Las Vegas, France, Acapulco, Bali, Macau, Germany and Kuala Lumpur, representing the ultimate innovation and commitment to excellence in adventure tourism.

6. **The Eiffel Tower** A 300 metre-high metal tower in Paris, completed in 1889. It is often used as a symbol representing Paris or France.

7. **Yo-Yo** A toy made of two circular parts that goes up and down a string that you hold in your hand.

## Language Points

1. **crane** *n.* a tall machine with a long arm, used to lift and move building materials and other heavy objects, a tall water bird with very long legs

2. **band** *n.* [C] a thin flat strip or circle of any material that is put around things

   papers held together with a rubber band

   a slim gold band on her finger

3. **tie sth to sth** to connect or link sth closely with sth else

   They tied him to a chair with cable.

   Her horse was tied to a tree.

4. **yonder** *pron.* (old use or dialect) over there

   the fresh blooms on yonder tree

   Let's rest under yonder tree.

5. **plunge** *v.* to move or make sb/sth move suddenly forwards and/or downwards

   Her car plunged off the cliff.

   Both the climbers had plunged to their deaths.

6. **ritual** *n.* a series of actions that are always carried out in the same way, especially as part of a religious ceremony

   the importance of religion and ritual in our lives

   The lady of the house performs the sacred ritual of lighting two candles.

   Set up a regular time for homework; make it a ritual.

   The ritual is performed in order to thank the Sun Goddess for the rice harvest.

   The book examines rituals for childbirth from different parts of the world.

7. **vine** *n.* any climbing plant with long thin stems

   I get beautiful vines and flowers, but eventually the flowers fall off and the stems turn brown and dry up.

Leaves brushed my face, a vine touched my arm and made me jump.

8. **cord**  n. [C,U]  strong thick string or thin rope, an electrical wire or wires with a protective covering, usually for connecting electrical equipment to the supply of electricity

   the phone cord, an extension cord

   The robe was held at the waist by a cord.

   He pulled explosives and some tangled cord from his bag.

9. **illegal**  adj.  not allowed by the law

   illegal drugs

   It is illegal to sell tobacco to children under 16.

   Large numbers of illegal immigrants crossed the border at night.

   Scott was arrested for being in possession of illegal drugs.

10. **gorge**  n.  a deep narrow valley with steep sides

    I saw a creek at one point, visible at the bottom of a gorge.

    It is well worth visiting just as a tourist or to do the five-hour walk along the bottom of the gorge.

    The wind blowing down the gorge was causing the boat to swing back and forth like a pendulum.

11. **make a deal**  when everyone agrees on a decision, plan etc.

    The local clubs are making every effort to interest more young people.

    The driver makes every effort to ensure the vehicle works well.

    They made a deal to sell the land to a property developer.

12. **fix up**  to arrange a meeting, event etc, to decorate or repair a room or building

    I fixed up an interview with him. We'll have to fix up a time to meet.

    We fixed up the guest bedroom before my parents came to stay.

13. **in return**  as payment or reward for something

    He is always helping people without expecting anything in return.

    Liz agreed to look after the baby in return for a free room.

    She gave us food and clothing and asked for nothing in return.

14. **dip**  v.  to put sth quickly into a liquid and take it out again

    He dipped his hand in the water. Dip the strawberries into melted chocolate.

    Emily dipped her toes in the water and squealed.

15. **bounce**  v.  if sth bounces or you bounce it, it moves quickly away from a surface it has just hit or you make it do this

    Two boys stood on the corner bouncing basketballs.

    First I thought that a bullet had hit me on the helmet and somehow bounced off.

16. **slam into**  to crash into sth with a lot of force; to make sth crash into sth with a lot of force

    All 155 passengers died instantly when the plane slammed into the mountain.

    **slam**  n.&v.  if a door, gate etc. slams, or if someone slams it, it shuts with a loud noise

    We heard a car door slam.

He slammed the door shut.

17. **add to**   to increase sth in size, number, amount, etc.

    Conforming to the new regulations will add to the cost of the project.

    The sales tax adds 8% to the price of clothes.

18. **triumph**   *n.* [U]   a great success, achievement or victory

    Winning the championship is a great personal triumph.

    Mary's final triumph was to see both of her boys go to college.

19. **tighten**   *v.*   if you tighten a rope, wire etc., or if it tightens, it is stretched or pulled so that it becomes tight

    When you tighten guitar strings, the note gets higher.

    The rope tightened around his body.

20. **spring**   *v.*   to move suddenly and with one quick movement in a particular direction

    Tom sprung out of bed and ran downstairs.

    Two men sprang out at me as I was walking through the park.

    He sprang to his feet (=stood up suddenly) and rushed after her.

21. **relieved**   *adj.*   feeling happy because sth unpleasant has stopped or has not happened

    She looked relieved when she heard the news.

    His mother was relieved to see him happy again.

    I felt relieved that Ben would be there.

## Answer Keys

### I. Getting the Message
1. C    2. A    3. A    4. B    5. B

### II. Developing Your Vocabulary

**Section A**

1. attached    2. originated    3. relieve    4. slammed    5. bounced    6. hooked

**Section B**

1. tied to       2. have a try       3. add... to
4. in return     5. slammed into     6. made a deal with

### III. Recognizing Main Ideas

1. have a try    2. originated    3. tied         4. named
5. tragedies     6. triumphs      7. relieved     8. unhooked

## IV. Trying the Translation

### Section A

1. 现代蹦极运动开始于 1979 年 4 月 1 日的英格兰。
2. 是一个新西兰人使蹦极成为一项大型运动。
3. 这个中心取得了巨大成功。
4. 对于许多人来说,危险只是增加了刺激性。
5. 也许有一天,你会去跳一下来分享这种快乐。

### Section B

1. Winning the championship is a great triumph.
2. Have a try—you might get the answer.
3. He is always helping people without expecting anything in return.
4. Tom sprung out of bed and ran downstairs.
5. The girl tied a scarf around her neck.

## V. Organizing Your Ideas

a e d c f b

## 参考译文

### 蹦 极

　　每个人都可以做到。爬上一幢高楼或吊车,或者到热气球上。有人会把一根粗粗的橡皮绳系在你的踝关节上,然后你就跳到空中。你的身体会向下面冲去,在最后时刻,橡皮绳会拉住你,你不会死的。

　　这项运动叫蹦极,起源于南太平洋上的岛国瓦努阿图。当地人是把蹦极作为一种男子汉仪式来进行的。他们把藤绳系在踝关节上,然后从竹楼上跳下。

　　现代蹦极运动开始于 1979 年 4 月 1 日的英格兰。那天正好是愚人节。牛津危险运动俱乐部成员想找一种新的刺激,所以他们就爬上高桥,把橡皮绳系在踝关节上往下跳。

　　然而,是一个新西兰人使蹦极成为一项大型运动。他的名字叫阿兰·约翰·海凯特。这个人胆子很大。有一次他竟从巴黎的埃菲尔铁塔上跳了下来。1988 年,他想让别人也尝尝蹦极的滋味。当时,这种运动是非法的,所以海凯特和新西兰警方达成一个协议。他自己出钱修复位于峡谷上的一座桥,作为回报,警方同意他在这座桥上开办一个蹦极中心。

　　这个中心取得了巨大成功。海凯特给每名蹦极者一件特殊的 T 恤衫。每个人都希望得到那样一件 T 恤衫。而且想得到的唯一条件是蹦极,越来越多的人同意这样做。一些蹦极者甚至做出了十分疯狂的举动。他们要求用一段特别长的绳索,这样在绳索拉住他们之前,他们能接触到河水。有个人把洗发水抹到头上,这样当他从河水中被拉起时,顺便就洗了头。

　　当然蹦极也存在危险。1989 年当两名法国蹦极者跳下时,他们的绳索断了,导致当场死亡。第三个人是因为撞上塔而死。但对许多人来说,危险只是增加了刺激性。而且蹦极者不谈论悲剧。他们谈论凯旋归来,谈论面对恐惧,谈论下降中的乐趣。在跳跃的过程中,速度可以达到每小时60英里。然后当绳子绷紧时,蹦极者像火箭一样重新被弹回空中。在很短的时间内,蹦极者像悠悠球一样在微风中上下弹跳。绳索没有弹性了,游戏也就结束了。

结束时蹦极者会感到高兴而又轻松。当从绳索上被解下来时,大部分人都会欢笑。许多人会大喊"嘿,看看我,我成功了!"也许有一天,你会去跳一下来分享这种快乐。

# ROCK CLIMBING

## Background Information

**Rock Climbing**  Although rock climbing was an important component of Victorian mountaineering in the Alps, it is generally thought that the sport of rock climbing began in the last quarter of the nineteenth century in various parts of Europe. Rock climbing evolved gradually from an alpine necessity to a distinct athletic activity.

Climbs can occur either outdoors on varying types of rock or indoors on specialized climbing walls. Outdoors, climbs usually take place on sunny days when the holds are dry and provide the best grip, but climbers can also attempt to climb at night or in adverse weather conditions if they have the proper training and equipment. Note that if a route freezes over completely and can no longer be climbed bare-handed, it would be more properly considered an ice climbing route instead.

### Styles of rock climbing

Most of the climbing done in modern times is considered free climbing—climbing using one's own physical strength with equipment used solely as protection and not as support—as opposed to aid climbing, the gear-dependent form of climbing that was dominant in the sport's earlier days. Free climbing is typically divided into several styles that differ from one another depending on the equipment used and the configurations of their belay, rope, and anchor systems (or the lack thereof).

***Bouldering*** is climbing on short, low routes without the use of the safety rope that is typical of most other styles. Protection, if used at all, typically consists of a cushioned bouldering pad below the route and/or a *spotter*, a person who watches from below and tries to break hazardous falls for the climber.

***Top roping*** is climbing with the protection of a rope that's already suspended through an anchor at the top of a route. A belayer controls the rope, keeping it taut, and prevents long falls.

***Lead climbing*** is climbing without the use of pre-set belays. One person (the leader) will start the climb carrying one end of the rope and will gradually attach it to additional anchors as he or she climbs, thereby establishing a belay system that progresses with the climb. The lead climbing article describes additional subtypes such as trad climbing and sport climbing.

***Free soloing*** (not to be confused with free climbing) is single-person climbing without the use of any rope or protection system whatsoever. If a fall occurs and the climber is not over water (as in the case of deep water soloing), the climber is likely to be killed or seriously injured. Though technically similar to bouldering, free solo climbing typically refers to routes that are far taller and/or far more lethal.

***Indoor climbing*** is climbing indoors (on a purpose-made climbing wall, typically), regardless of the style(s) used.

## Language Points

1. **steep**　*adj.*　(of a slope, hill, etc.) rising or falling quickly, not gradually
   *To my right lies a steep slope.*
   *The road became rocky and steep.*

2. **comment**　*n.*　sth you say or write which gives an opinion on or explains sb/sth
   *Are there any questions or comments?*
   *He made some comment about my dress, then carried on reading his book.*
   *Her comments on interest rates had little impact on financial markets.*

3. **be addicted to**　spending all your free time doing sth because you are so interested in it
   *I tried to give up smoking several times before I realized I was addicted.*
   *It's quite easy to get addicted to drugs.*

4. **grovel**　*v.*　to move along the ground on your hands and knees, especially because you are looking for sth
   *I looked back and saw him grovelling in the road for his hat.*
   *I had to really grovel to the bank manager to get a loan.*
   *I grovelled to my parents and promised I wouldn't do it again.*

5. **gruesome**　*adj.*　very unpleasant and filling you with horror, usually because it is connected with death or injury
   *a gruesome murder*
   *gruesome pictures of dead bodies*
   *We spent a week in a gruesome apartment in Miami.*

6. **scare**　*v.*　to frighten sb
   *The alarm scared the hell out of me. He was driving fast just to scare us.*
   *It scared him to think that his mother might never recover.*
   *She scared the hell out of me when she said she had to go into hospital.*
   **be scared out of your wits**　to be very frightened

7. **wit**　*n. [U, sing.]*　the ability to say or write things that are both clever and amusing
   *have a quick wit*
   *a woman of wit and intelligence*

8. **route**   n.   a way that you follow to get from one place to another

   the most direct route home

   We weren't sure about which route we should take.

   If you don't enjoy driving on the main highways, try some of the rural routes.

9. **scenery**   n. [U]   the natural features of an area, such as mountains, valleys, rivers and forests, when you are thinking about them being attractive to look at

   The best part of the trip was the fantastic scenery.

   The train passes by some breathtaking scenery in the Canadian Rockies.

   We stayed in a peaceful Alpine village surrounded by magnificent scenery.

10. **breathtaking**   adj.   very exciting, spectacular

    The view from my bedroom window was absolutely breathtaking.

    The changes in the city since 1980 have been breathtaking.

    The drive along the beach and up the mountain and is truly breathtaking.

    The guest house was on the side of the cliff, with breathtaking views of the ocean below.

11. **surroundings**   n. [pl.]   all the objects, conditions, etc. that are around sb/sth; environment

    He switched on the light and examined his surroundings.

    I need to work in pleasant surroundings.

    It took me a few weeks to get used to my new surroundings.

12. **ultimate**   adj.   final, better, bigger, worse etc than all other things or people of the same kind, most extreme

    The ultimate aim is to replace gasoline altogether by using battery power or other non-polluting energy sources.

    Human welfare is the ultimate goal of economic activity.

    For many people, the Rolling Stones will always be the world's ultimate rock and roll band.

13. **depend on**   to be affected or decided by sth

    The country depends heavily on its tourist trade.

    We depend entirely on donations from the public.

    **depend on sb/sth for sth**

    Many women have to depend on their husbands for their state pension.

    **depend on sb/sth to do sth**

    I'm depending on you to tell me everything.

    **depend on sb/sth doing sth**

    We're depending on him finishing the job by Frida.

14. **adapt to**   to change your behavior in order to deal more successful with a new situation

    The children are finding it hard to adapt to the new school.

    After living in a house with a garden, it's hard to adapt to living in a flat.

    Slowly the country is adapting to the new market economy.

15. **adventure**   n. [C]   an unusual, exciting or dangerous experience, journey or series of events

    All right, I'll go without you—you guys have no sense of adventure at all!

As a young man he went off to Africa, looking for adventure.

He always used to tell us about his adventures at sea.

16. **count on**  to trust sb to do sth or to be sure that sth will happen

    We're all counting on winning this contract.

    They were counting on him not coming out of hospital.

    You've got to understand that we can't count on the Shah any more.

17. **bond**  *n. [C]*  something that forms a connection between people or groups, such as a feeling of friendship or shared ideas and experience

    Over the years the two men had developed deep bonds of friendship.

    The bond between mother and child is extremely strong.

18. **slope**  *n.*  a surface or piece of land that slopes (= is higher at one end than the other)

    a slope of 30 degrees

    The car rolled down the slope into the lake.

19. **instruction**  *n. [pl.]*  the written information that tells you how to do or use something, *[C]* order or direction given , *[U]* formal teaching that you are given in a particular skill or subject

    Install the machine according to the manufacturer's instructions.

    Press enter and follow the on-screen instructions.

20. **fundamental**  *adj.*  serious and very important

    Raising your child to tell the difference between right and wrong is one of the fundamental tasks of parenthood.

    Water is fundamental to survival.

# Answer Keys

## I. Getting the Message

### Section A

1. N    2. NG    3. Y    4. Y    5. Y    6. Y

### Section B

1. climbing up very steep rock surfaces
2. Once you have picked up rock climbing
3. scare the wits out of you
4. but about balance
5. an individual, social
6. save your life some day

## II. Recognizing Main Ideas

1. are addicted to    2. boring    3. routes    4. come across    5. adventure
6. fit                7. both      8. ride      9. moves         10. instruction

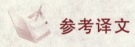

参考译文

## 攀 岩

攀岩是一项攀登悬崖峭壁的运动。为什么要去攀岩呢?谈到攀岩,人们说的第一句话就是:你疯了吗?那样做太危险了!但是千万不要让这些说法阻止你尝试的脚步。一旦你尝试过,你就会了解为什么会有那么多人对攀岩如此着迷了。

究竟为什么这么多人要把攀岩作为自己的爱好呢?比起攀岩来,还有其他更容易的方式可以达到目的啊!毕竟在攀岩过程中,你有时会划破双手,而且通常会遍体鳞伤,有时候你甚至会被吓得魂飞魄散。既然如此,为什么还是有那么多人攀岩呢?

攀岩绝不会让人感到乏味。攀登的线路实在太多。当攀岩者寻找新的攀岩路线时,他总会意外欣赏到各种美景和自然风光。另外,要记住:一旦你到达山顶,你将欣赏到令人叹为观止的美景,这样的景致是绝大多数人无法看到的。

挑战体能极限——每天行走在岩石上是提高自己现有技术的好机会。因此,每次攀岩的时候,你都应该尽力去提高自己的技能。去尝试新的、更困难的路线,依靠自己的体能和承受风险的能力,你会发现没有什么级别的攀岩是不可征服的。同时,攀岩者们从中得到的正是一种冒险和自由的感觉。随时随地去自己想去的地方,这种感觉真是太棒了!

然而攀岩并不只是与体力有关。它与身体的平衡能力,你对自己身体的了解程度以及你在空中不断调整身体位置的能力有关。同时它与创造力有关,即适应不同岩石状况的能力。攀岩是一项全身运动,虽然上半身起着很重要的作用,但是腿和脚却是帮助你向上移动的最重要的部位。另外,它还与注意力有关。只有集中注意力你才能克服置身悬崖峭壁的恐惧感。

选择攀岩作为爱好,你不一定要年轻或者特别适合这项运动。许多人是年纪很大才开始攀岩的,并且各个年龄层次都有优秀的攀岩手。据我所知,有些超过50岁的攀岩选手甚至可以和年轻人比拼。

攀岩既是一项个人运动也是一项团体运动。当你在岩石上攀爬时,你可能只靠自己的技能就可以到达山顶,然而,当你失足时,你必须信赖你的攀爬伙伴。这样一来就造就了牢固的团队关系。

学习攀岩和学习骑自行车或学习雪坡滑雪极其相似。你要始终记得那些基本动作要领,但是要使这些技能达到完善的程度,需要通过多年的努力。

对于所有高级别的攀岩来说,得到正确的指导是至关重要的。去找一家攀岩俱乐部或学校学习吧。正确的指导很可能有一天会挽救你的生命。

# Reading in Focus

## 识别主题句 Locate the Topic Sentences

*Direction: Find and underline the topic sentences in the following paragraphs.*

1. The center was a huge success.
2. Spanish is spoken in many countries.
3. There are many cooking utensils in my kitchen.
4. Dogs in US are treated like humans.

# Unit Eight

## Stagecraft

###  Script for Lead-in Listening

Listen to the following conversation and fill in the blanks with the correct words or phrases. You may choose the words or phrases from the list given.

Maria: What are we going to see this evening?
Wang: There's Beijing Opera, a concert and Chinese acrobatics. What do you prefer?
Maria: Oh, they all sound interesting. It's hard for me to decide.
Wang: Have you ever seen Beijing Opera before?
Maria: No, never.
Wang: Then I'd recommend it. It's one of our major traditional operas with a history of 200 years. It's something special you've probably never seen before.
Maria: I've not heard much about it but I do know that it's unique to Chinese culture.
Wang: The basic types of performance include singing, reciting, acting and fighting.
Maria: That's interesting if a little confusing for me.
Wang: Look at these pictures. They show some wonderful performances given both at home and abroad.
Maria: Wow. That's great. I just can't wait to see it.

### WORDS AND PHRASES IN LEAD-IN LISTENING

**acrobatics**  *n.*  acrobatic acts and movements
  Her acrobatics were greeted with loud applause.
**recommend**  *v.*  to tell sb that sth is good or useful, or that sb would be suitable for a particular job, etc.
  I recommend the book to all my students.
  The hotel's new restaurant comes highly recommended (= a lot of people have praised it).
**prefer**  *v.*  to choose one thing rather than sth else because you like it better
  I prefer jazz to rock music.
  "Coffee or tea?" ——"I'd prefer tea, thanks."
**unique**  *adj.*  belonging to or connected with one particular person, place or thing
  Several holidays are unique to America.
  The custom is unique to the region.

**performance**  n.  the act of performing a play, concert or some other form of entertainment
   *It's one of the band's live performances.*
**recite**  v.  to say aloud a poem, piece of literature, etc. that you have learned, especially to an audience
   *My little daughter likes reciting poetry in public.*

# TEXT A

# BEIJING OPERA

## Background Information

**1. Beijing Opera (Peking Opera)**  It has existed for over 200 years. It is widely regarded as the highest expression of the Chinese culture. It is known as one of the three main theatrical systems in the world. Artistically, Beijing Opera is perhaps the most refined form of opera in the world. It has deeply influenced the hearts of the Chinese people. Although it is called Beijing Opera, its origins are not in Beijing but in the Chinese provinces of Anhui and Hubei. Beijing Opera got its two main melodies, xipi and erhuang, from Anhui and Hubei operas. It then absorbed music from other operas and musical arts in China.

It is regarded that Beijing Opera was born when the Four Great Anhui Troupes (四大徽 帮) came to Beijing in 1790. Beijing Opera was originally staged for the royal family and came into the public later. In 1828, some famous Hubei Troupe players came to Beijing. Hubei and Anhui troupes often jointly performed in the stage. The combination gradually formed the mainstream of Beijing Opera's melodies. One of the rare forms of entertainment, it was favored by people from all walks of the society, from the high-ranking government officials to the lower levels of society. There are thousands of pieces covering the entire history and literature of China, even including revised stories from the west.

There are as many kinds of Chinese Opera as there are dialects. It has been estimated that there are thousands branches of Chinese Opera. Most of them are local, dominating a region within a province and its surrounding area. However, Beijing Opera is the national standard, and has a higher reputation than any of the other branches of Chinese Opera. Almost every province of China has more than one Beijing Opera troupe. Beijing and Tianjin are respected as the key base cities in the north while Shanghai is the base in the south.

Due to the threat from other entertainments, Beijing Opera's out-of-date styles and the lack of historical and theatrical knowledge of the young, this art lost a lot of its audiences. Most of the audiences are old people, who were children when Beijing Opera was at its peak. The art is dying.

There have been campaigns and efforts to rescue this and other theatrical arts. The Chinese Opera journal has sponsored the annual Plum Blossom Award (梨花奖) for more than ten years. Each year, the journal invites dozens of opera and drama players to perform in a Beijing theater. The award goes to those who top the poll conducted by the journal. Winners, who must be younger than 45, include actors and actresses from all around China. A Plum Blossom Chinese painting was selected as the Award's official symbol. Other performance competitions among the young actors and actresses have been screened live and aired in China Central Television (CCTV), the largest TV network in China, and national radio stations. Following outstanding Peking Opera performers including Mei Lanfang (梅兰芳), Cheng Yanqiu (程砚秋), Ma Lianliang (马连良), Zhou Xinfang (周信芳) and Du Jinfang (杜近芳), the emergence of many young artists has continued to breathe new life into Peking Opera.

2. **Martial Art**  Chinese martial art is one of the most well known elements of traditional Chinese culture. The origin of Chinese martial art can be dated back to the earliest age. It combines theories of self-defense and health-keeping. Chinese martial art is rich in numerous styles. They can be divided in two categories: external (Shaolin 少林, Wudang 武当) and internal (Tai Ji Quan 太极拳, Qigong 气功) and also includes the practice of many weapons (sword, stick, spear...). Quite confidential in Europe before the Sixties, Bruce Lee's (李小龙) movies then made it very popular among western countries.

3. **Hanju (Hubei Opera** 汉剧**)**  One of the ancient local operas in Hubei Province, China, enjoys a history of more than 300 years. It has great influence on Beijing opera, Chuanju (川剧), Dianju (滇剧), Qianju (黔剧), Guiju (桂剧), Ganju (赣剧), Xiangju (湘剧) and Guangdong (Cantonese) Yueju operas (粤剧).

4. **Kunqu (Kunshan Opera)**  One of the earliest forms of traditional Chinese drama, having a history of more than 600 years. Its operatic melodies originate from Kunshan in Jiangsu Province. After extensive exploration and reworking by its performers, it gradually developed into today's Kunqu. In 2001, UNESCO for the first time awarded the title of "Masterpieces of the Oral and Intangible Heritage of Humanity" to 19 outstanding cultural forms of expression from different regions of the world. Kunqu Opera was among them.

5. **Sheng**  The male role in Beijing Opera. Sheng, according to the age, personality and status of the characters, is subdivided into laosheng, xiaosheng, wensheng and wusheng. Laosheng, also known as xusheng, is a bearded middle-aged or old man who is in most cases a positive character. Xiaosheng is a handsome young man, who can either be a scholar or a military general. Those who specialize in singing and reciting are termed wensheng, while those who are skilled in stage-fighting, are called wusheng.

6. **Dan**  A general term in Beijing Opera for all female roles. In the feudal society of old China, as men and women were forbidden to perform on the same stage, all the female roles were played by men. According to the age, status, personality of the character and the style in acting, dan is further divided into zhengdan, huadan, caidan, wudan and laodan. Zhengdan is also called qingyi because she always wears a qingyi (black costume). Zhengdan is the type representing the gentle and virtuous young and middle-aged woman. In this type of roles

much stress is given in singing. Huadan is the role for a maiden or a young woman, who is either lively or clever in character. Emphasis is placed on acting and recitation in this type. Caidan, also called choudan, is the role for a woman of comical or crafty character. A caidan uses heavy make-up of rouge with a patch of white powder covering her nose while her acting is basically the same as that of a chou (clown). Wudan is the role for a woman of the military type who excels in riding and martial arts. Like wusheng, a wudan does a lot of stage-fighting. Laodan is the role for an old woman. In singing laodan uses the natural voice which is similar to laosheng. In both singing and acting the performer must try to indicate the special characteristics of an old woman.

7. **Jing**  It is also known as hualian, a role with a painted face, who is a man of special character, features and personality. Jing is further divided into wenjing (civilian type) and wujing (warrior type). Wenjing must lay particular emphasis on singing and wujing on acrobatic fighting. The face of a jing role is painted with a variety of coloured patterns which are not only an artistic exaggeration but also an indication of the personality of the character.

8. **Chou**  It is also called xiaohualian or sanhualian. A chou (clown) may be a kind-hearted, humorous and funny fellow. However, he may also be very wicked or deceptive. Chou is also divided into wenchou (civilian type), and wuchou (a clown with martial arts). A female chou is normally called caidan or choudan. A chou always paints his nose powder-white and wears an upturned moustache so as to give a comic effect.

## Language Points

1. **comprehensive**   *adj.*   including all, or almost all, the items, details, facts, information, etc., that may be concerned

   This is the largest and most comprehensive study ever made of the city's social problems.
   Our company offers the customers a comprehensive service to meet all their needs.
   The nuclear plant was given a comprehensive inspection before being declared safe.

2. **pantomime**   *n. [C, U, usually sing.]*   the use of movement and the expression of your face to communicate sth or to tell a story

   A most amusing pantomime was acted before her.
   The children were very excited by the pantomime.

3. **prevail**   *v.*   to exist or be very common at a particular time or in a particular place

   Old traditions still prevail in the mountainous area.
   Justice will prevail over injustice.
   Virtue will prevail against evil.

4. **know no limit**   to have not a point at which sth stops being possible or existing

   He knows his own limits.
   Her ambition knows no limit.

5. **portray** *v.* to describe of show sb/sth in a particular way, especially when this does not give a complete or accurate impression of what they are like

   Lady Macbeth is portrayed as an evil woman.
   Her book portrays her father as a cruel man.
   He portrayed King Lear in the play.

6. **symbolize** *v.* to be a symbol of sth

   The poet has symbolized his lover with a flower.
   The statue symbolizes progress and peace.
   For me, this experience symbolizes the process kids and parents go through.

   **symbolic** *adj.* containing symbols, or being used as a symbol

   The dove is symbolic of peace.

7. **in a word** (*spoken*) used for giving a very short, usually negative, answer or comment

   Would you like to help us? In a word, no.
   In a word, I am tired of everything.
   In a word, we should solve this problem by ourselves.

8. **accompaniment** *n.* [C, U] music that is played to support singing or another instrument

   He sang to a piano accompaniment.
   The election results were announced to the accompaniment of loud cheering.

9. **refer to sb/sth** to describe or be connected to sb/sth

   It can also refer to a long-term occupation.
   It can refer to an academic subject or a practical skill.

10. **subdivide (sth) (into sth)** to divide sth into smaller parts; to be divided into smaller parts

    Part of the building has been subdivided into offices.
    The house is being subdivided into apartments.

11. **civilian** *adj.* of a person who is not a member of the armed forces or the police

    Their new plan is to attack civilian targets.
    He resigned to take up a civilian job.

12. **comic** *adj.* [only before noun] connected which comedy (= entertainment that is funny and that makes people laugh)

    His jokes brought some comic relief to a very dull party.
    The play is a good means for his comic talent.

13. **at first sight** when you first begin to consider sth

    At first sight, it may look like a generous offer, but in fact not.
    I fell in love with her at first sight.
    Not judge men and things at first sight.

14. **impress sb (with sb/sth)** if a person or thing impresses you, you feel admiration for them or it

    She impressed us all with her intellectual powers.
    It's vital to impress the consumer with a good advertising campaign.
    I was greatly impressed by the handiness with which she played the piano.

15. **resemblance**  *n.* [C, U]  the fact of being or looking similar to sb/sth

    The children have a great resemblance to their parents.

    She bears little resemblance to her mother.

    Mars is all the more interesting for its close resemblance to our earth.

    **resemble**  *v.*  to look like or be similar to another person or thing

    She closely resembles her sister.

    So many hotels resemble each other.

16. **nobility**  *n.*  people of high social position who have titles such as that of duke or duchess

    Congress may not grant titles of nobility.

    The houses of the nobility were forbidden to the common man.

17. **upright**  *adj.*  (of a person) behaving in a moral and honest way

    He is an upright citizen.

    We are upright in our business.

18. **besides**  *prep.*  in addition to sb/sth; apart from sb/sth

    Any student of this school must learn one more foreign language besides English.

    Besides dieting, taking exercise plays a part in losing weight.

    Besides intelligence and charm, Mary had some less desirable qualities.

19. **reform**  *v.*  to improve a system, an organization, a law, etc. by making changes to it

    A series of reform experiments have been done.

    Eastern European governments have finally accepted the need to reform.

    He raised some proposals to reform the party.

20. **eliminate**  *v.*  to remove or get rid of sth/sb

    We'll have to eliminate unnecessary waste.

    They announced that they will eliminate 9,300 jobs.

    It can eliminate most of the dust and particles.

21. **feudal**  *adj.*  connected with or similar to feudalism

    The feudal influence is still strong in China.

    Women found the feudal conventions too strong for them to break away from.

22. **emerge**  *v.*  to start to exist; to appear or become known

    After the elections opposition groups began to emerge.

    He emerged as a key figure in the campaign.

23. **on the basis of**  to be grounded on/upon

    On the basis of new information, police have arrested a man at the airport.

    She was chosen for the job on the basis of her ideas.

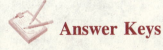

# Answer Keys

### I. Getting the Message

1. A    2. B    3. D    4. C    5. C

## II. Developing Your Vocabulary

### Section A
1. comprehensive
2. portray
3. symbolize
4. prevail
5. reforming
6. eliminate

### Section B
1. In a word
2. refers to
3. at first sight
4. subdivide into
5. impressed with
6. resemblance to

## III. Recognizing Main Ideas
1. characterized
2. symbolic
3. tunes
4. local
5. painted
6. colorful
7. embroidery
8. reforms

## IV. Trying the Translation

### Section A
1. 京剧是集音乐、歌唱、对白、哑剧、杂技和武术于一体的综合表演艺术。
2. 京剧舞台无时空限制。
3. 京剧的角色依照不同的性别、年龄、社会地位和职业分为四大行当。
4. 京剧的服装色彩鲜明,刺绣精美,令观众印象深刻。
5. 在传统京剧流派的基础上,新一代的年轻演员已经涌现并正在取得新的成就。

### Section B
1. Jack is hard-working and intelligent. In a word, I can't speak too highly of him.
2. They undertook a comprehensive survey of the city's problems.
3. What I have to say refers to all of you.
4. States are subdivided into counties.
5. The children have a great resemblance to their parents.

## V. Organizing Your Ideas
d  a  e  c  f  b

# 参考译文

## 京 剧

京剧是集音乐、歌唱、对白、哑剧、杂技和武术于一体的综合表演艺术。

京剧中盛行使用象征手法。京剧舞台无时空限制,适于表演任何动作。演员的表演大多是哑剧。台步、手势及各种各样的身体运动可表现和象征开门、爬山、上楼或划船等动作。四位将军和四名士兵可代表数千人的军队。总之,京剧演员的每一动作都具有高度的象征意义。

京剧的音乐结合了徽剧二黄调,汉剧(湖北戏剧)西皮调以及昆曲(昆山戏剧)的曲调和伴奏。京剧的伴奏使用中国特有的乐器,二弦琴京胡和二胡是其中两种主要乐器。

京剧的角色依照不同的性别、年龄、社会地位和职业分为四大行当。生指男性角色,可再分为老生(中老年男性角色)、小生(青少年男子角色)、武生(有武艺的男性角色)。旦指女性角色。旦和生一样可分为不同类型。青衣指道德观念严肃的女性角色;花旦指活泼的年轻女性;武旦指有武艺的女性角色;而老旦指老年女性角色。净指面部化妆的角色,通常是武士、英雄、政治家甚至神怪。净可再分为文净和武净。丑是喜剧角色,可通过其特有的面部化妆(鼻子上方的一块白色油彩)一眼辨认出来。丑可再分为文丑和武丑。

京剧的服装色彩鲜明,刺绣精美,令观众印象深刻。现在表演用的一些服装同明朝(1368—1644)的风格非常相似。不同颜色可表明不同的社会地位——黄色指皇室、红色指高官、红色或蓝色指正直的人,白色指老年官员、黑色可用于每个角色。通常书生穿蓝袍、将军戴甲胄、皇帝穿龙袍。除了色彩鲜明的服装和头饰,京剧中的男性角色还使用饰有宝石的腰带而女性角色使用各种头部装饰品。

解放后,在改革这一传统戏剧方面取得了很大成就。在消除封建因素、提高舞台技巧和拓宽戏剧主题方面做出了很多努力。在传统京剧流派的基础上,新一代的年轻演员已经涌现并正在取得新的成就。

## FACIAL MAKEUPS

 **Background Information**

**1. Nuo** (傩)　A time-honoured cultural phenomenon of rituals practiced to drive out evil spirits and diseases. Its name is derived from one such rituals, where people shouted "Nuo, Nuo" to drive away the devil. From temples, masks, dramas, symbols and costumes, to weapons, nuo culture is a complex mix of anthropology (人类学), ethnicity (种族划分), folk customs(民间习俗), religious ceremonies and dramatic values. Knowing about nuo culture gives a quick glance at the primitive and mysterious ways of ancient Chinese. China is preparing to name nuo as an Intangible Cultural Heritage through UNESCO.

In its prime, nuo was popular across the country. Nuo dance (傩舞) is known as the "living fossil of Chinese dance." Nuo drama is an intelligent creation of working people, and nuo masks continue to stir imagination and inspiration.

The nuo dance was originally performed to drive away evil spirits at sacrificial rituals during ancient times. The nuo ceremony was first recorded on bones and tortoise shells during the Shang Dynasty (16th-11th century BC, 商朝), and flourished in the Zhou Dynasty (11th century—256 BC, 周朝). As the number of its participants increased from 100 to 1,000, ceremonies became more magnificent. At the time, besides the grand nuo ceremony held by the royal court, nuo folk ceremonies also appeared in the countryside.

With the development of science and technology, the dance gradually declined, and in the Central Plains in the middle and lower reaches of the Yellow River, it disappeared completely after the Song Dynasty (960-1279, 宋朝). Today, the dance can only be seen during the Spring Festival in remote mountainous areas, such as parts of Guizhou, Hunan, Yunnan, Sichuan, and Anhui provinces, inhabited mostly by minority ethnic groups.

2. **Prince Lanling** (?~573)   Prince Lanling Gao Changgon (高长恭) or Gao Su (高肃) is the grandson of Emperor Gao Huan (高欢) and son of Emperor Gao Cheng (高澄). He was killed by his cousin, Emperor Gao Wei (高纬) when he was only about 28 years old.

## Language Points

1. **frighten**   *v.*   to make sb suddenly feel afraid

    *Sorry, I didn't mean to frighten you.*

    **frighten sb/sth off/away (from sth)**   to make a person or an animal go away by making them feel afraid

    *He threatened the robbers with a gun and frightened them off.*

2. **relieve**   *v.*   to remove or reduce an unpleasant feeling or pain

    *Being able to tell the truth at last seemed to relieve her.*

    *His jokes relieved the tension in the room.*

3. **transform sb/sth (from sth) (into sth)**   to completely change the appearance or character of sth, especially so that it is better

    *The company has been transformed from a family business to an international company.*

    *The photochemical reactions transform the light into electrical impulses.*

4. **theatrical**   *adj.*   connected with the theatre

    *There are two beautiful theatrical performances this evening.*

    *He comes from a theatrical family.*

5. **excel in/at sth/at doing sth**   to be very good at doing sth

    *She has always excelled in foreign languages.*

    *The team excels at turning defence into attack.*

    *As a child he excelled at music and art.*

6. **terrorize**   *v.*   to frighten and threaten people so that they will not oppose sth or will do as they are told

    *Drug dealers terrorize the neighborhood*

    *Thousands of people were terrorized into leaving their homes.*

7. **overwhelm**   *v.*   to defeat sb completely

    *The army was overwhelmed by the rebels.*

    *Our team overwhelmed the visitors by 40 points.*

8. **bring onto the stage**  to organize and present a play or an event for people to see

    *They brought a tragedy on the stage*

    *This new play has been brought onto stage.*

9. **as well (as sb/sth)**  in addition to sb/sth; too

    *They sell books as well as newspapers.*

    *She is a talented musician as well as being a teacher.*

10. **undoubtedly**  *adv.*  used to emphasize that sth exists or is definitely true

    *There is undoubtedly a great deal of truth in what he says.*

    *The performance is undoubtedly a success.*

11. **bearing**  *n. [U]*  the way in which sth is related to sth or influences it

    *Recent events had no bearing on our decision.*

    *Regular exercise has a direct bearing on fitness and health.*

12. **portrayal**  *n. [C,U]*  the act of showing or describing sb/sth in a picture, play, book etc.; a particular way in which this is done

    *The article examines the portrayal of the statesmen in the media.*

    *He is best known for his portrayal of Hamlet.*

13. **standardize**  *v.*  to make objects or activities of the same type have the same features or qualities; to make sth standard

    *Efforts to standardize English spellings have not been completely successful.*

    *Many of the standardized tests in use today can be traced back to it.*

    *The parts of an automobile are standardized.*

14. **spring up**  to appear or develop quickly and/or suddenly

    *Play areas for children are springing up all over the city.*

    *New houses were springing up all over the town.*

    *Doubts have begun to spring up in my mind.*

15. **perfect**  *v.*  to make sth perfect or as good as you can

    *As a musician, she has spent years perfecting her techniques.*

    *They have perfected the art of winemaking.*

16. **finalize**  *v.*  to complete the last part of a plan, trip, project, etc.

    *They met to finalize the terms of the agreement.*

    *You should finalize your plans/arrangements.*

17. **by means of**  (*formal*) with the help of sth

    *The load was lifted by means of a crane.*

    *They succeeded by means of patience and sacrifice.*

18. **limit sth to sth**  to stop sth from increasing beyond a particular amount or level

    *We should take measures to limit the production of waste gases from cars.*

    *The amount of money you have to spend will limit your choice.*

19. **be characterized by**  [often passive] to give sth its typical or most noticeable qualities or features

    *The city is characterized by tall modern buildings in steel and glass.*

The giraffe is characterized by its very long neck.
Flu is a disease characterized by fever and pains.
Developing countries are characterized by a widening gap between the rich and the poor.

20. **variety**  *n. [sing.]*  several different sorts of the same thing
There is a wide variety of pictures to choose from.
He left for a variety of reasons.
This tool can be used in a variety of ways.

## I. Getting the Message

### Section A
1. Y  2. N  3. Y  4. N  5. Y  6. NG

### Section B
1. relieve people of diseases.
2. overwhelm the enemy.
3. had a bearing on
4. became finalized.
5. praise or dispraise toward the characters.
6. the disposition of the character.

## II. Recognizing Main Ideas
1. peculiar   2. originate   3. ancient   4. reputed   5. springing up
6. made   7. leads   8. highlight   9. quality   10. appreciated

## 脸谱艺术

中国戏剧中的脸谱艺术历史悠久。古时候人们在傩祭仪式上表演傩舞来恫吓邪神恶鬼，祛除疾病。傩舞表演者跳舞时都戴假面，后来在一些地区傩舞仪式变成了一种戏剧表演。戴假面的另一例子是北齐时期的兰陵王。据说兰陵王武艺出众，但容貌俊美难以威吓敌人，所以作战时总戴面相凶恶的假面以震慑敌人。这一传说在南北朝及隋唐时期被搬上舞台。傩祭者和表演艺术中所使用的面具毫无疑问与脸谱的起源有关。唐朝的艺术家开始在扮演神鬼时直接在脸上勾画。明朝时在元朝基础上对表演者行当的区分更为分门别类，戏剧与脸谱逐步规范化。清朝时期，随着京剧的兴起，脸谱艺术进一步完善。不同类别的人物脸谱在清朝末期最终定型。

脸谱是中国戏剧的特有艺术,通过艺术的夸张再结合真实的表演和象征手法,既明确表现不同角色的扮相,也表明其性情与道德品质。脸谱也用于表现对不同角色的褒贬。

京剧中使用一千多种脸谱图案。每一种脸谱图案的作用就在于它能对已定的脸谱图案做出细微有趣的改变。脸谱在某些地方戏剧中被应用于所有不同的角色,但在中国戏剧的代表——京剧中脸谱只限于净角和丑角。丑角以涂白的鼻子为特征来获取一种戏剧效果。京剧中丑角的脸谱图案很少,但有大量的净角脸谱图案,如"整脸、四分脸、六分脸"等。

脸谱中使用不同的颜色如红、黄、蓝、白、黑、紫、绿、金、银。脸谱的主色象征人物的性情。如红色表示忠勇正直,金银两色常用于鬼神。

脸谱不仅是中国戏剧的特有艺术,还是一种装饰设计艺术,已成为中国画的一个新的分支。

# Reading in Focus

## 阅读特定信息——定义 Reading for a Definition

定义能准确揭示事物的本质特征,在英语阅读中必须注意定义这一特定信息。在 Text A 和 Text B 中,有更多的下定义的例子。

**1. 使用谓语动词或动词短语下定义进行解释**

用于下定义的谓语动词或动词短语有 be, mean, deal with, be considered, to be, refer to, be called, be known as, define, represent, signify, constitute 等。

例如:

**Laodan** *is an elderly woman.* (Text A)

**Facial makeups** *are a special art in Chinese operas which distinctly show the appearances of different roles as well as their dispositions and moral qualities by means of artistic exaggeration combined with truthful portrayal and symbolism.* (Text B)

**Sheng** *is the male role in Beijing Opera.*

**Facial makeups** *are not only a special art in Chinese operas, but also an art of ornamental design, and have become a new variety in Chinese painting.* (Text B)

**Xiaosheng** *is a handsome young man, who can either be a scholar or a military general.*

**Dan** *is a general term in Beijing Opera for all female roles.*

**Zhengdan** *is the type representing the gentle and virtuous young and middle-aged woman.*

**Huadan** *is the role for a maiden or a young woman, who is either lively or clever in character.*

**Wudan** *is the role for a woman of the military type who excels in riding and martial arts.*

**Laodan** *is the role for an old woman.*

**Dan** *refers to female roles.*

**Zhengdan** *is also called qingyi because she always wears a qingyi.*

**Laosheng**, *also known as xusheng, is a bearded middle-aged or old man who is in most cases a positive character.*

*...those who are skilled in stage-fighting are called* **wusheng.**

**Caidan**, *also called choudan, is the role for a woman of comical or crafty character.*

**Jing** *is also known as hualian, a role with a painted face.*

*A female chou is normally called* **caidan** *or* **choudan.**

其他例子：

*A* **territory** *is an area that an animal, usually the male, claims as its own.*

由定义可推知，这里 territory 指的是："动物的地盘"。

*The term "***arts***" usually refers to humanities and social sciences.*

**Anthropology** *is the scientific study of man.*

由定义可知，anthropology 就是"研究人类的科学"，由此可推出 anthropology 是"人类学"。

**Insomnia** *is the inability of falling asleep.*

表语的意思是"不能入睡或睡不着"，那么主语 insomnia 无疑就是"失眠"。

**Wrestling** *is the game which is played by two strong people; one player tried to get the other down on the floor.*

通过后面的定义解释：Wrestling 是"两人进行的，彼此尽力把对方弄倒在地的比赛"，可以猜出 wrestling 是"摔跤，摔角"。

*The word "***adolescence***" means the period between children and adulthood.*

adolescence 是生词，但我们根据它的定义可以猜出其含义："青春期"。

## 2. 使用定语从句下定义进行解释

*The* **herdsman**, *who looks after sheep, earns about 650 yuan a year.*

定语从句中 looks after sheep 就表明了 herdsman 的词义为"牧人"。

*He takes a special interest in* **botany** *which concerns the study of plants.*

根据定语从句中 which concerns the study of plants 可知 botany 是"植物学"。

*Tom suffers from* **SAD**, *which is short for seasonal affective disorder.*

根据生词 SAD 后面定语从句 which is short for seasonal affective disorder，可以推断出 SAD 含义，即"季节性情绪紊乱症"。

**Procrastinators** *are people who have a chronic habit of putting things off, usually until the last minute and sometimes until it is too late altogether.*

定语从句 who have a chronic habit ... altogether 是说 procrastinator 是一种具有推迟办事的缓慢习气的人，通常拖到最后时刻，有时甚至误了大事，不难猜出该词为"办事拖拉的人"。

*Headlines often contain relatively unusual words like "***blaze***", which is often used instead of "fire".*

定语从句说"blaze"常常代替"fire"使用,这说明 blaze 与 fire 同义。

**3. 使用同位语下定义进行解释**

1) 使用标点符号引出定义

构成同位关系的两部分之间多用逗号连接,有时也使用括号、冒号、分号、引号和破折号等标点符号引出定义进行解释。

The music of Beijing Opera combines the erhuang tune from Anhui Opera, the xipi tune from **Hanju** (*Hubei Opera*), and tunes and musical accompaniment of **Kunqu** (*Kunshan Opera*).

Sheng is subdivided into **laosheng** (*middle-aged or old men*), **xiaosheng** (*young men*) and **wusheng** (*men with maritial skills*).

Jing can be further divided into **wenjing** (*civilian type*) and **wujing** (*warrior type*).

Chou is subdivided into **wenchou** (*civilian clown*) and **wuchou** (*clown with martial skills*).

其他例子:

The doctor was on the **night-shift** — *from midnight to 8 o'clock.*

这里 night-shift 的意思可以由破折号后面的内容猜出,意思是"夜班"。

**Semantics**, *the study of the meaning of words*, is necessary.

此例逗号中短语意为"对词意义进行研究的学科"。该短语与前面生词 semantics 是同位关系,因此不难猜出 semantics 指"语义学"。

The Greek marriage was **monogamous**—*men and women were allowed only one spouse at a time.*

破折号后面的文字是对 monogamous 的解释,即"一夫一妻制"。

The purpose of the campaign was to catch "**ringers**", *students who take test for other students.*

同位语 students who take test for other students(替他人考试)是对 ringers 作解释的,因此 ringers "代考者"的意思就不难悟出了。

They finally got to a **castle**, *a large building in old times.*

同位语部分 a large building in old times 给出了 castle 的确切词义,即"城堡"。

In fact, only about 80 **ocelots**, *an endangered wild cat*, exist in the US today.

由同位语 an endangered wild cat 我们很快猜出生词 ocelots 的义域:"一种濒临灭绝的野猫"。

2) 利用注释性词语引出定义

所谓注释性词语,就是为进一步补充说明前述内容而承上启下的过渡性词语,如使用 or, similarly, that is to say, in other words, namely, including, meaning, or other, say, i.e. 等副词或短语来引出定义。

Numbers such as 1, 2, 3, 4, 10, 100 are called whole numbers, or **integers**.

integer 是生词,但从整个句子来看,integers 其实就是"whole numbers"(整数)的同位语,所以 integer 的意思是:"整数"。

It will be very hard but also very **brittle**, *that is, it will break easily.*

从后面的解释中我们可以了解到 brittle 是"脆"的意思。

**Capacitance**, *or the ability to store electric charge*, is one of the most common characteristics of electronic circuits.

由同位语我们很快猜出生词 capacitance 的词义"电容量"。

He is a **pedant**, *in other words, a person who lays too much stress on book-learning*.

通过 in other words(换句话说)引起的下文是解释 pedant 的意思,根据下文阐述的内容"太注重书本知识的人",那就是"书呆子"或"学究"。

Newspaper headlines are short, for example, "**gems**" *meaning "jewels"*, "**bid**" *in the sense of "attempt"*.

meaning 后面的词就是其前面的词的意思, bid 就是 attempt 的意思。

They are **vertebrates**, *that is, animals that have backbones*.

这里 vertebrates 的意思可以由 that is 后面的内容猜出,意思是"脊椎动物"。

I. **Direction: Find the definitions of the following terms from the texts according to the reading skills you have learnt in this unit.**

1. female roles.
2. the roles with painted faces.
3. a clown with martial arts.
4. a form of dance performed at ritual ceremonies in ancient China
5. one of the ancient local operas in Hubei Province, China

II. **Direction: Rewrite the following sentences by giving definitions to the italicized parts according to the tips in the brackets.**

1. *Chou* refers to a clown.
2. They finally got to a *castle*, which is a large building in old times.
3. The *herdsman*, who looks after sheep, earns about 3,000 yuan a year.
4. *Jing*, a role with a painted face, is subdivided into wenjing and wujing.
5. He is a *pedant*, in other words, a person who lays too much stress on book-learning.

# Keys to Test Two

**Tape scripts for Listening Comprehension**
**Part I Listening Comprehension**
**Section A (12 points)**

1. W: Can I see Zulu on Sunday?
   M: I'm not sure.
   Q: When does the woman want to see Zulu?

2. W: Bill, that's a lovely painting in your living room!
   M: I'm glad you like it. It's a Christmas gift from my son.
   W: Well, it's beautiful. Your son has very good taste!
   Q: What are the speakers talking about?

3. W: Excuse me. I'm looking for Mr Tang.
   M: Oh, he is not on this floor. He is on the fourth floor, go down the stairs and turn left.
   Q: Where are the two speakers now?

4. M: Do you like football?
   W: Yes, very much.
   M: Would you like to go to a match on the 18th of December?
   Q: Which of the following statements is not correct about the woman?

5. W: I like organ music. Do you know where I can hear a recital?
   M: Try St. Mary's Church. I know they have a beautiful organ.
   Q: What does the man know about St. Mary's Church?

6. W: Do you think you could stop whistling? I'm trying to write an essay.
   M: Oh, I'm sorry. I thought you were in the other room.
   Q: What was the woman trying to do?

7. M: What are you going to do after the lesson?
   W: I'm probably going to have a cup of tea. What about you?
   M: Oh, I'm going to the post office.
   Q: Where is the man probably going after the lesson?

8. M: Do you have to play that music so loud? I've got a test tomorrow!
   W: Sorry, I didn't realize you were studying.
   Q: What will the woman probably do?

9. M: So, how is your new roommate?
   W: She really makes me angry.
   M: What happened?
   W: She's always making loud noises at midnight. When I remind her, she's always rude.
   Q: What can we learn from the conversation?

10. M: Did you go to the meeting yesterday evening?
    W: I planned to, but my mom was't feeling well, so I had to be home with her.
    Q: What did the woman do yesterday evening?

11. W: Oh, Tom, you don't look well. Are you OK?
    M: No, I was sick most of the night. I didn't sleep much.
    W: Did you have a cold or something?
    M: No. It was just the cold meal I had on the train.
    Q: What is the most probable cause of the man's sickness?

12. W: Terry, do you have any time for coffee? I'd like to get your opinion about our new product design and its market.
    M: Sure. I've been giving it some thought lately and I have a few ideas I'd like to talk to you about.
    Q: What are the two speakers going to do?

## Section B (10 points)

My family and I lived in a flat until last spring. We weren't happy there. The building was crowded and noisy, and the manager didn't fix things. We decided to move. But most flats in this city were even worse, and the cost was higher. So we started to look for a house to buy. Finally, my husband and I found a small house not far away from the city center. The problem was the house itself. It was ugly. It needed paint. The wallpaper was old; the carpet was in terrible condition, and it was orange. The door and roof needed repairs. The "garden" was full of dirt and a few half-dead plants. When our children first saw their new home, they burst into tears. I understood that. I wanted to cry myself. Well, the four of us made a decision to share the work and spend our summer vacation on the house. We fixed the door and the roof. We changed the ugly wallpaper and carpet. We planted trees and grass. Day by day, this terrible little house became our home. We're happy there now. The children are quite satisfied, except for one thing—now it's their job to cut the grass every weekend.

# Keys to Test Two

**Part I Listening Comprehension**

**Section A (12 points)**

1. B   2. D   3. C   4. C   5. A   6. D   7. A   8. A   9. B   10. A   11. D   12. C

**Section B (10 points)**

1. flat   2. crowded   3. worse   4. problem
5. wallpaper   6. condition   7. half-dead   8. tears
9. to share the work and spend our summer vocation on the house
10. We moved the ugly wallpaper and carpet.
11. now it's their jib to cut the grass every weekend

**Part II Reading Comprehension (30 points)**

1-5 DDCCC   6-10 ADBCD   11-15 ACDDB   16-20 DBDDC

**Part III Vocabulary & Structure (12 points)**

1-5 DCCCC   6-10 CBDCB   11-15 CADAA   16-20 DBDCB   21-24 DCBD

**Part IV Cloze (10 points)**

1-5 DBDCB   6-10 DACBD   11-15 DABCD   16-20 BACDA

**Part V Translation**

**Section A (10 points)**

1. 高价使许多顾客望而却步。
2. 教授历史不应该局限于讲年代和人物。
3. 本培训课程将使你能胜任更好的工作。
4. 儿童游乐场所如雨后春笋般地在这个地方四处出现。
5. 大峡谷永远让人叹为观止。

**Section B (10 points)**

**Direction: Translate the following sentences into English, using the words or phrases in the brackets.**

1. In view of the weather,
2. at a rate of 12 million per year.
3. adapt oneself to life in different cultures.
4. Having been addicted to computer games,
5. In order to afford my education,

**Part VI Organizing Your Ideas (6 points)**

b   e   a   d   f   c

113

# Unit Nine

# Sports in China

 ## Script for Lead-in Listening

Listen to the following conversation and fill in the blanks with the correct words or phrases. You may choose the words or phrases from the list given.

(A coach is cheering up a tennis player after her defeat in a game.)

**Linda:** Sorry, Mr Black. I really don't know what's wrong with me.

**Mr Black:** Come on, Linda. Don't cry.

**Linda:** Sorry, I just can't help...

**Mr Black:** Calm down, girl. Have some water. Now, let's talk about the game. What do you think about how it went?

**Linda:** Well, I should have done better, Mr Black. I prepared well and I thought I was completely ready.

**Mr Black:** Well, you played a good game and you stuck to your game plan.

**Linda:** I really don't know what else I could have done.

**Mr Black:** You made a few mistakes and your opponent jumped at them.

**Linda:** She really played a perfect game today.

**Mr Black:** She sure did. But don't be sad. You'll have a chance to play her later in the season. I'm sure you can beat her if you improve.

**Linda:** Thanks, Mr Black. I'll try my best.

## WORDS AND PHRASES IN LEAD-IN LISTENING

**season** *n.* a period of time during a year when a particular activity happens or is done
   *He scored his first goal of the season on Saturday.*

**improve** *v.* to make sth/sb become better
   *I need to improve my English.*

**calm down** *v.* to become or make sb become not excited, nervous, or upset
   *Look! Calm down! We'll find her.*

**stick to sth** *v.* to continue doing or using sth and not want to change it
   *She finds it difficult to stick to a diet.*

# TEXT A

# SPORTS IN CHINA

 **Background Information**

1. **The Olympic Games**  An international multi-sport event subdivided into summer and winter sporting events. The summer and winter games are each held every four years. Until 1992, they were both held in the same year. Since then, they have been separated two years apart.

   The International Olympic Committee was founded in 1894 on the initiative of a French nobleman, Pierre Frédy, Baron de Coubertin. The first of the IOC's Olympic Games were the 1896 Summer Olympics, held in Athens, Greece. Participation in the Olympic Games has increased to include athletes from nearly all nations worldwide.  With the improvement of satellite communications and global telecasts of the events, the Olympics are consistently gaining supporters.  The most recent Summer Olympics were the 2004 Games in Athens and the most recent Winter Olympics were the 2006 Games in Turin. The upcoming games in Beijing are planned to comprise 302 events in 28 sports.  As of 2006, the Winter Olympics were competed in 84 events in 7 sports.

2. **NBA**  The national Basketball Association, an organization of professional ballplayers in the US and Canada that decides rules and organizes competitions

3. **The Nationwide Physical Fitness Program**  The "Physical Health Law of the People's Republic of China" was adopted in 1995. In the same year, the State Council announced the "Outline of Nationwide Physical Fitness Program", followed by a series of rules and regulations. Aiming to improve the health and the overall physical condition of the general population, the Nationwide Physical Fitness Program, with an emphasis on young people and children, encourages everyone to engage in at least one sporting activity every day, learn at least two ways of keeping fit and have a health examination every year. In this 15 year long program, the government aims to build a sport and health-building service system for the general public. The Nationwide Physical Fitness Program has set targets that, by 2010, about 40 percent of China's population will participate in regular physical exercise, there will be a clear improvement in the national physique and a major increase in the number of fitness sites so as to satisfy people's needs for keeping fit.

## Language Points

1. **associate sb/sth with sb/sth**  to make a connection between people or things in your mind
   The study found that many people associate science with masculinity.
   He no longer wished to be associated with his past.

2. **competitive**  *adj.*  used to describe a situation in which people or organizations compete against each other
   He quit playing competitive football at the age of 26.
   Graduates have to fight for jobs in a highly competitive market.

3. **expert**  *n.* [C]  a person with special knowledge or skill or training in sth
   He is an expert at getting his own way.
   Don't ask me! I'm no expert.

4. **estimate**  *v.*  to form an idea of the cost, size, value etc. of sth, but without calculating it exactly
   We estimated that it would cost about $3,000.
   It is estimated that the project will last for three years.

5. **urban**  *adj.*  [only before noun] connected with a town or city
   People moved to the urban areas for jobs.
   Urban poverty is on the increase.

6. **prominent**  *adj.*  important or well known
   He played a prominent part in the campaign.
   She was prominent in the fashion industry.

7. **prior to**  [only before noun] happening or existing before something else, before a particular event
   The questions had been asked prior to my arrival.
   All should be finished during the week prior to the meeting.

8. **fund**  *v.*  to provide money for sth usually sth official
   The museum is privately funded.
   This programme is government-funded.

9. **quit**  *v.*  to leave one's job, school, etc.
   He has decided to quit as manager of the team.
   If I don't get more money, I'll quit.

10. **carry out**  to do and complete a task
    Extensive tests have been carried out on the patient.
    The building work was carried out by a local contractor.

11. **come into being**  to start to exist
    The Irish Free State came into being in 1922.
    Do you know when the earth came into being?

12. **emergence**  *n.* [U]  the process of appearing or becoming recognized
    With the emergence of English as the medium of international communication, English

*becomes more and more popular.*

*The cause for the island's emergence from the sea is still a mystery.*

13. **participate**   v.   to take part in an activity or event

    *We want to encourage students to participate fully in the running of the college.*

    *The rebels have agreed to participate in the peace talk.*

14. **bid**   n. [C]   an effort to do sth or to obtain sth

    *Do you think he'd be willing to mount another bid for the presidency?*

    *The company cut prices just before Christmas in a bid to support sales.*

15. **so as to do sth**   with the intention of doing sth

    *The Athletics Federation has introduced stricter regulations so as to prevent cheating.*

    **so... as to**   to such a degree

    *I am not so stupid to believe that.*

# Answer Keys

## I. Getting the Message
1 D    2. B    3. D    4. A    5. C

## II. Developing Your Vocabulary

### Section A
1. participate    2. competitive    3. professionalize
4. estimated      5. prominent      6. emergence

### Section B
1. came into being    2. is being carried out/has been carried out    3. prior to
4. associated with    5. so as to                                      6. a variety of

## III. Recognizing Main Ideas
1. associated       2. popular    3. a number of    4. professionalization
5. have done well   6. held       7. succeeded      8. bid

## IV. Trying the Translation

### Section A

1. 传统的中国文化认为身体健康是一个很重要的方面。20世纪以来,包括西方的和中国传统的形式在内的大量的体育活动在中国普及。

2. 1994年这种情况开始转变。当时,中国足球第一个走上职业化的道路,篮球、排球、乒乓球、围棋也进行了类似的改革。

3. 体育协会变成了盈利的实体,俱乐部体制形成。

4. 北京奥组委成立于2001年底,确立2008奥运会的主题为"绿色奥运"、"科技奥运"、"人文奥运"。

5. 除竞技体育外，中国还致力于全民健康和整体身体素质的提高。

**Section B**

1. Guo Jingjing is one of the athletes trained for the Olympic Games.
2. He made a desperate bid to escape from his attackers.
3. It is estimated that about 60 percent of the students in our school participate in regular physical exercise.
4. During the week prior to the final, the coach fell ill.
5. He played a prominent part in the competition yesterday.

## V. Organizing your ideas

b  e  c  d  a  f

## 中国的体育

尽管长期以来人们把中国和武术联系在一起，但是，今天的中国体育指的是在包括中国内地、香港、澳门在内的中国境内所进行的各种竞技体育运动。传统的中国文化认为身体健康是一个很重要的方面。20世纪以来，包括西方的和中国传统的形式在内的大量的体育活动在中国普及。在每四年举办一届的夏季奥运会上，中华人民共和国是成绩最好的国家之一，在许多项目上表现突出，如乒乓球、羽毛球、跳水、体操。足球与乒乓球一起成为今天的中国最受欢迎的运动，类似的情况在中国已经有两千年的历史。某位专家估计在中国13亿人口中有多达5亿人踢足球或观看足球比赛。篮球和一些其他运动项目在中国也越来越受欢迎，尤其是在城市。对于许多人，尤其是老年人，传统的体育活动，如太极拳和气功仍然是日常生活的一部分。在中国，板球也是一种受人欢迎的运动，但是，在香港情况更是如此，在那里板球是一种重要的体育运动。

在20世纪90年代以前，与其他一些国家一样，中国的体育完全由政府资助。一些顶尖的运动员在事业的巅峰期离开，因为他们对退役后的生活没有把握。1994年这种情况开始转变。当时，中国足球第一个走上职业化的道路，篮球、排球、乒乓球、围棋也进行了类似的改革。这一过程带来了商业化，体育协会变成了盈利的实体，俱乐部体制形成，职业联队出现，改善了中国的体育环境，商业管理体制形成。体育的职业化促进了体育管理市场和商业结构体制的出现。改革的另一个方面是中国的运动员也加入了国外的职业联队。如篮球明星姚明加入了NBA的球队。

在1949年中华人民共和国成立前，中国运动员参加了三届奥运会，但没有取得任何奖牌。自从1949年以来，中国已经参加了六届夏季奥运会和七届冬季奥运会，并在夏季奥运会上获得112枚金牌。2001年7月，北京最终成功获得2008年奥运会的举办权。北京奥组委成立于2001年底，确立2008年奥运会的主题为"绿色奥运"、"科技奥运"、"人文奥运"。

除竞技体育外，中国还致力于全民健康和整体身体素质的提高。全民健身项目已经确立目标：到2010年为止，约40%的中国人将定期参加体育锻炼，全民体魄将有明显的提高，健身场所将大幅度增加以满足人民健身的需要。

## FOOTBALL GAMES OF OLD CHINA

### Background Information

1. **The Han Emperor Wu Di** (156BC-87BC), personal name Liu Che (刘彻), was the seventh emperor of the Han Dynasty in China, ruling from 141 BC to 87 BC. Emperor Wu is best remembered for the vast territorial expansion that occurred under his reign, as well as the strong and centralized Confucian state he organized. He is cited in Chinese history as one of the greatest emperors. Emperor Wu's reign lasted 54 years—a record that would not be broken until the reign of the Kangxi Emperor (康熙皇帝) more than 1800 years later.

2. **Cuju** The game of cuju was first mentioned in Sima Qian's Shiji (司马迁的《史记》), written during the Han Dynasty. Some historians claim that the Yellow Emperor (黄帝) invented the game for military training purposes, while others place its emergence during China's Warring States Period (476-221 BC)(战国时期). A competitive form of cuju was used as fitness training of soldiers, while other forms were played for entertainment in wealthy cities like Linzi (临淄).

   During the Han Dynasty (206 BC-AD 220), the popularity of cuju spread from the army to the royal courts and upper classes.

   Cuju flourished during the Song Dynasty (960-1279) due to social and economic development, extending its popularity to every class in society. At that time, professional cuju players were quite popular, and the sport began to take on a commercial edge.

   Cuju organizations were set up in large cities called Qi Yun She (齐云社), or Yuan She (圆社)—now known as the earliest professional cuju club-whose members were either cuju lovers or professional performers.

   Cuju began its decline during the Ming Dynasty (1368-1644) due to neglect, and the 2,000-year-old sport slowly faded away.

3. **Huo Qubing** (140 BC-117 BC), born in Linfen, Shanxi, was a general of the western Han dynasty under Emperor Wu. Being the illegitimate son of Wei Shaoer (卫少儿), he was the nephew of Wei Qing (卫青) and Empress Wei Zifu (卫子夫).

   Although raised in reasonable prosperity during the early glory days of the Wei family, he exhibited outstanding military talent as a teenager. When he was 20 years old, he and Wei Qing were sent with separate armies to attack the Xiongnu on the largest-scale Han offensive to date. He was greatly rewarded for his efforts.

   Though a brave general and highly regarded by Emperor Wu, he paid little regard to his men. Sima Qian noted in Shiji that Huo Qubing refused to share his food with his soldiers when their provisions were low, and also regularly ordered his troops to dig up football fields for his personal amusement. However, when it came to martial glory, Huo Qubing never hesitated to share the honor with his men. One of the most famous tale is that when Emperor Wu awarded Huo a jar of precious wine for his achievement, he poured it into a creek so all his troopers drinking the water could share a taste of it. This tale gave rise to the name of the city Jiuquan (酒泉).

Huo Qubing died at the early age of 24 due to a plague, possibly the result of a primitive form of biological warfare.

**4. The Hexi Corridor** (The Gansu Corridor)    It refers to the historical route in Gansu province of China. As part of the Northern Silk Road running northwest from the bank of the Yellow River, it used to be the most important passage from ancient China to Central Asia for traders and the military. As early as the first millennium BC, silk goods began appearing in Siberia having traveled over the Northern Silk Road including the Hexi Corridor segment. The ancient trackway formerly passed through Haidong, Xining and the environs of Juyan Lake (居延海), seving an effective area of about 215,000 km$^2$. It was an area where mountain and desert limited caravan traffic to a narrow trackway where fortification could control who passed.

More specifically, Hexi is a long narrow passage stretching for about 1000 km from the steep Wushaolin hillside near the modern city of Lanzhou to the Jade Gate (玉门关) at the border of Gansu and Xinjiang. There are many fertile oases along the path. The strikingly inhospitable environment surrounds them: the vast expanse of the Gobi desert, the snow-capped Qilian Mountains to the south, the Beishan mountainous area (北山地区), and the Alashan Plateau (阿拉善高原) to the north.

**5. The Xiongnu**    A nomadic people from Central Asia. "Xiongnu" was the most ancient name that was given to the Turkic tribes of Central Asia by the Chinese. They appear in Chinese sources from the 3rd century BC as controlling an empire (the "Asian Hun Empire " under Modu Shanyu (冒顿单于) stretching beyond the borders of modern day Mongolia. They were active in the areas of southern Siberia, western Manchuria (满洲) and the modern Chinese provinces of Inner Mongolia, Gansu, and Xinjiang. Relations between the Han Chinese and the Xiongnu were complicated and included military conflict, exchanges of tribute and trade, and marriage treaties.

**6. Song Emperor Huizong** (November 2, 1082—June 4, 1135)    The eighth and one of the most famous emperors of the Song Dynasty of China, with a personal life spent amidst luxury and art but ending in tragedy.

Born Zhao Ji (赵佶), he was the 11th son of Emperor Shenzong (神宗). In February 1100 his older half-brother Emperor Zhezong (哲宗) died childless, and Huizong succeeded him the next day as emperor. He reigned from 1100 to 1126.

Huizong was famed for his promotion of Taoism. He was also a skilled poet, painter, calligrapher, and musician. He sponsored numerous artists at his court, and the catalogue of his imperial painting collection lists over 6,000 known paintings.

## 💡 Language Points

1. **inflate**　*v.*　to fill sth or become filled with gas or air
   The pump inflated the tyres automatically.
   Inflate your life jacket when necessary.

2. **attest**　*v.*　to show or prove that sth is true
   He has found a witness who would attest the signature.
   She can attest to the fact.

3. **pitch**　*n.* [U]　(BrE) (AmE **field**) an area of ground specially prepared and marked for playing a game such as football
   Hundreds of fans invaded the pitch at the end of the game.
   The rugby pitch is government-funded.

4. **referee**　*n.* [C]　the official who controls the game in some sports, such as football, basketball and boxing
   He was sent off for arguing with the referee.
   Referees should be respected when they are on duty.

5. **deputy**　*n.* [C]　a person who is the next most important person below a business manager, a head of a school, a political leader, etc. and who does the person's job when he or she is away
   Mr Smith is the deputy head of the school.
   I'm acting as deputy till the manager returns.

6. **nurture**　*v.*　to help sb/sth to develop and be successful
   The magazine has a reputation for nurturing young writers.
   It's important to nurture a good working relationship.

7. **acquaint sb/yourself with**　to make sb familiar with or aware of sth
   Please acquaint me with the facts of the case.
   You will first need to acquaint yourself with the rules.

8. **reverse**　*adj.*　[only before noun] opposite to what has been mentioned
   You can reverse the jacket so that the pattern is on the outside.
   Writing is reversed in a mirror.

9. **take turns (in sth/to do sth)**　(BrE **take it in turns**) if people take turns or take it in turns to do sth, they do it one after another to make sure it is done fairly
   We take turns to do the housework.
   The couple took turns to cook.

10. **appropriate**　*adj.*　suitable, acceptable or correct for the particular circumstances
    This isn't the appropriate time to discuss the problem.
    We need to ensure the teaching they receive is appropriate to their needs.

11. **flog**  *v.*  to punish sb by hitting them many times with a whip or stick

    He was publicly flogged for breaking the law.

    Flogging is a kind of punishment still used in some countries.

12. **smother**  *v.*  to cover sth / sb thickly or with too much of sth

    She smothered him with kisses.

    The meat was smothered in thick sauce.

13. **incorporate sth (in/into/within sth)**   to include sth so that forms a part of sth

    Many of your suggestions have been incorporated in the plan.

    The government incorporated this principle into the 1977 law.

14. **festive**  *adj.*  typical of a special event or celebration

    The decorations gave the room a festive air.

    The whole town is in festive mood.

15. **decline**  *v.*  to become smaller, fewer, weaker, etc.

    Her health was declining rapidly.

    Support for that party continued to decline.

# Answer Keys

## I. Getting the Message

### Section A
1. Y    2. N    3. Y    4. N    5. Y    6. NG

### Section B
1. hair and other soft fillings
2. chief and deputy
3. military training
4. reverse kick-basketball
5. the golden age
6. festive occasions

## II. Recognizing Main Ideas

1. inflated    2. team    3. performed    4. training    5. entertainment
6. reached    7. enjoyed    8. different    9. popular    10. declined

## 参考译文

### 中国古代的足球

　　足球,更确切地说是英式足球,第一次出现是在中国的汉朝(公元前206年—公元220年)。正如现在的足球一样,当时的足球用皮子制成,里面填充头发或其他柔软的填充物,而不是充气。据说汉武帝喜欢这项运动。当时,蹴鞠由军队传到宫廷和上流社会。或许令人惊讶的是这项运动在这个国家有如此漫长的历史,而更让人感到惊讶的是参加这项运动的有男子和女子。这一点在汉朝的历史记载和石刻中可以得到证实。当时这项运动注重的是个人技巧而非团队技巧。

　　汉朝的足球场地四面有围墙。每一方有12名队员,还有主裁判和副裁判共两名裁判员。研究汉朝的学者们认为足球,又称蹴鞠(字面意义即踢球)是一种有效的军事训练形式。它有助于强健体魄、鼓舞士气、使士兵熟知进攻和防御的技巧。例如,汉代大将霍去病率领军队到河西走廊与匈奴入侵者作战时,下令修建足球场地、进行足球运动。

　　在唐朝(618—907)女子足球运动员又一次出现,此时,足球是用8块皮缝制在动物膀胱外,球内充气。女子在这项运动中技艺高超。这项运动其实是一种反向的踢篮球。双方队员轮流向挂在球场中央的一个单独的悬空的球门射门。球门建在两个10米高的柱子上,两个柱子之间挂有一个球网,球网的一面有直径一米的开口。

　　紧随其后的宋朝(960—1279)被认为是中国蹴鞠的黄金时代。足球在单球门和双球门的场地进行,但是后一种成为全国喜爱的一种方式,在宫廷和普通百姓中都受到欢迎。足球制作工艺有所改进,球壳由12块皮而非8块皮制成,使得球体更圆。

　　宋徽宗生日庆贺的一个重要方面是皇室球队间的比赛。在这种场合下,两名裁判的裁决一定要非常恰当,因为输了的球队将面临杖刑并且脸上还将被涂上厚厚的黄色和白色的粉末。足球比赛最终成为一种风俗习惯,在喜庆场合进行。在所有参赛者喝下第六杯酒的时候比赛开始。这种比赛更具有表演性而非竞技性,比赛也不像在宋徽宗生日庆贺时那样激烈。

　　蹴鞠在元朝(1279—1368)和明朝(1368—1644)时仍然盛行,但是在清朝(1644—1911)走向衰落。

### 英语阅读猜词技巧 Guess the Meaning of a Word

**1. 根据词的构成猜测词义**

　　我们可以研究一下词的构成,看是否可以把词拆开,找出词的前缀、后缀和词根。分析了各个构成成分的意思之后,通常这个词的意义就会变得清楚起来。如:

　　Compact discs (CDs) are an example of a form of supertechnology which was nonexistent be fore microchips made it possible to store macro-amounts of data in miniscule space.

在这句话里面,好多词的词义可以根据其构成猜测出来:

supertechnology:super-(超级的)+technology(技术)=超级技术

nonexistent:non-(否定前缀)+exist(存在)+-ent(形容词后缀)=不存在的

microchip:micro-(微小的)+chip(小片)=微型芯片

macro-amount:macro-(巨大的)+amount(数量)=大量

2. 根据同义词线索猜测词义

通过同义词猜词,一是要看由 and 或 or 连接的同义词词组,如 happy and gay,即使我们不认识 gay 这个词,也可以知道它是愉快的意思;二是看在进一步解释的过程中使用的同义词,如 Man has known something about the planets Venus, Mars, and Jupiter with the help of spaceships. 此句中的 Venus(金星)、Mars(火星)、Jupiter(木星)均为生词,但只要知道 planets,就可猜出这几个词都属于"行星"这一义域。

3. 根据反义词线索猜测词义

有的时候你可以猜出一个生词的意思,因为它正好是文中某个事物的对立面。如:

In many nations there are two financial extremes, from penury to great wealth.

我们知道,penury 和 great wealth 是经济状况的两个极端(two financial extremes),因此它们是一组反义词,由于 great wealth 是"非常富有",那么 penury 就是"非常贫穷"。

4. 寻找解释生词的句子

有的时候,包含有生词的句子的前面的句子或后面的句子会解释这个生词。如:

Mary's personality-her enthusiasm, her lively actions, her excitement at new ideas -always attracted people. I never know such an ebullient woman.

第一个句子中的 enthusiasm, lively actions, excitement at new ideas 可以帮助我们理解 ebullient 的含义,即"热情洋溢的"、"热烈奔放的"。

5. 根据同位语线索猜测词义

有的时候,作者会预料到有些词在读者的阅读中会构成困难,因此会用简单的、常见的词给予解释。这是一种非常常见的解释方法。我们可以通过标点符号(如逗号、破折号等)或通过信号词(如 or, that is, meaning 等)来找到同位语部分。如:

例如:But sometimes, no rain falls for a long, long time. Then there is a dry period, or drought.

从 drought 所在句子的上文我们得知很久不下雨,于是便有一段干旱的时期,即 drought,由此可见 drought 意思为"久旱","旱灾"。这种同义或释义关系常由 is, or, that is, in other words, be called 或破折号等来表示。

6. 根据自己的经验和常识猜测词义

人类的感受和情感都有一定的通性,而语言也有逻辑性,所以有的时候,我们可以通过自己的经验和常识来猜测词义。如:

Feeling depressed, Carmella began to cry.

我们知道,一个人通常不高兴时才会哭,所以把 depressed 猜成 unhappy 应该没有大错。

7. 通过例子来猜测词义

有的时候,我们可以对文中所举出的例子进行归类,从而归纳出该集合名词的词义。如:

Don't eat too many dairy foods (milk, butter and cheese).

由于牛奶、黄油和奶酪都与奶有关,所以可以推测出dairy的意思为"牛奶的"、"乳品的"。

I. Direction: Guess the meaning of the italicized words. Tell what technique(s) you have used.

1. 副手,常识推理　　　　2. 责备,因果关系　　　　3. 不英俊,反义关系

4. 任意处置、用完即丢,词缀分析 (disposable=dis+pos+able,其中 pos=place,put;dis=apart;able 表示能够)

5. 动物,举例

II. Direction: Read the following passage and guess the meaning of the italicized words.

1. 手腕(或身体的某一部分)　　2. 撞击　　3. 专业人士　　4. 特技演员
5. 把戏　　　　　　　　　　　6. 爆炸　　7. 受伤　　　　8. 悬崖

# Unit Ten

# Cartoon Stars

## Script for Lead-in Listening

Listen to the following conversation and fill in the blanks with the correct words or phrases. You may choose the words or phrases from the list given.

Jo: Hello, Jo speaking.
Bill: This is Bill. Listen, Jo I won't have to work tomorrow. I can take you sightseeing.
Jo: That's very kind of you. It's my first time here. I'd like that. Where will you take me?
Bill: We could start with Disney Paradise. It's quite near here.
Jo: What's interesting about it?
Bill: You'll be able to view the cartoon films.
Jo: That sounds good!
Bill: And you can play with the cartoon stars.
Jo: Wonderful!
Bill: You can even play the part of one of the cartoon stars.
Jo: Wow! Can I get dressed up as Donald?
Bill: Sure! You can act as any one you like.
Jo: Maybe I'll find out if I have the ability to be a cartoon star.
Bill: I'm afraid you won't. You've never performed in a play before, have you?

### WORDS AND PHRASES IN LEAD-IN LISTENING

**sightseeing**  *n.*  the activity of visiting interesting buildings and places as a tourist
  Did you have a chance to do any sightseeing?

**start with**  at the beginning
  I'll have melon to start with.

**view**  *n.*  What you can see from a particular place or position, especially beautiful natural scenery
  There were magnificent views of the surrounding countryside.

**play the part of**  to act the role of sb
  He had always wanted to play the part of Othello.

**dress up**  to put on special clothes, especially to pretend to be sb/sth different
  Kids love dressing up.
  The boys were all dressed up as pirates.

# TEXT A

## CREATION OF STARS

### Background Information

1. **Walt Disney**  Hollywood feared new technology—but Disney used it to create an iconic brand—Mickey Mouse. Three years later, Disney added color to his growing menagerie, which included Minnie, Goofy, and Donald Duck. And in 1937, he made Hollywood's first full-length animated film, Snow White and the Seven Dwarfs, a $1 million production that nearly bankrupted the company he and his older brother Roy had established in 1923.

   The man whose name is an American icon was born in Chicago in 1901, a farmer's son. Disney's first business, making satirical cartoons in Kansas City, went bust, so with $500 from an uncle, he and Roy headed for Hollywood, where they started a small studio. Walt Disney Studio was fueled by Walt's imagination. Disney forever altered entertainment with his bet on Disneyland, built in 1955 on a 182-acre citrus grove in Anaheim, Calif. Not long after, The Mickey Mouse Club was born, and the driving force of the company became cross-promotion. Disneyland's Frontierland gave rise to the Davy Crockett TV series that in turn created a national craze for coonskin caps - licensed by Disney.

   Expansion continued after Walt's death in 1966 at age 64. The 28,000 Florida acres Disney purchased for $5 million opened as Walt Disney World's Magic Kingdom six years later. Kids flock to Disney parks from Paris to Tokyo—and today buy Mickey DVDs on their way out the gates.

2. **Charles Schulz**  Born in Minneapolis, Minnesota, and grew up in Saint Paul. He was the only child of Carl Schulz, who was German, and Dena Schulz attended St. Paul's Richard Gordon Elementary School, where he skipped two half-grades.

   After his mother died in February 1943, he was drafted into the United States Army and was sent to Fort Campbell in Kentucky. After leaving the army in 1945, he returned to Minneapolis where he took a job as an art teacher. His first regular cartoons, Li'l Folks, were published from 1947 to 1950 by the St. Paul Pioneer Press; he first used the name Charlie Brown for a character there, although he applied the name in four gags to three different boys and one buried in sand. The series also had a dog that looked much like Snoopy. In 1948, Schulz sold a cartoon to the Saturday Evening Post; the first of seventeen single-panel cartoons by Schulz that would be published there. Later that year, Schulz approached the United Feature Syndicate with his best strips from Li'l Folks, and Peanuts made its first appearance on October 2, 1950. The strip became one of the most popular comic strips of all time.

   Schulz's family returned to Minneapolis and stayed until 1958. They then moved to Sebastopol, California, where Schulz built his first studio. In 1966, his Sebastopol studio burned down. By 1969, Schulz had moved to Santa Rosa, California, where he lived and worked for more than 30 years.

3. **Chuck Jones**  In a career spanning over 60 years, Jones made more than 300 animated films, winning three Oscars as director and in 1996 an honorary Oscar for Lifetime Achievement. Among the many awards and recognitions, one of those most valued was the honorary life membership from the Directors Guild of America.

Born on September 21, 1912 in Spokane, Washington, Jones grew up in Hollywood where he worked occasionally as a child extra in Mac Sennett comedies. Then, in 1932, he got his first job in the fledgling animation industry as a cell washer for former Disney animator, Ubbe Iwerks. It was at Iwerks Productions that he met Dorothy Webster, to whom he was married in 1932.

In 1936 Jones was hired by Friz Freleng as an animator for the Leon Schlesinger Studio (later sold to Warner Bros.). In 1937 his daughter, Linda, was born, and in 1938 he directed his first film, The Night Watchman.

When Warner Bros. closed, Jones moved to MGM Studios, where he created new episodes from the Tom and Jerry cartoon series. Jones established his own production company, Chuck Jones Enterprises, in 1962 and produced nine half-hour animation films for television including Rudyard Kipling's Rikki Tikki Tavi and The White Seal.

In 2000, Jones established the Chuck Jones Foundation, designed to recognize, support and inspire continued excellence in art and the art of classic character animation.

## Language Points

1. **brawn**  *n.* [U]  physical strength

    *In this job you need brains as well as brawn.*

    *He was both the brains and the brawn of this film.*

    **brains and brawn**  in the text means that Charles Schulz was both the sponsor and the animator of the Peanuts comics.

2. **panel and strip**  small drawings in a row of a cartoon sequence

3. **syndicate**  *v.*  [usually passive] to sell an article, a photograph, a television programme, etc. to several different newspapers, etc.

    *His column is syndicated throughout the world.*

    *He is the most widely syndicated cartoonist in history.*

4. **decide upon sth**  to choose sth from a number of possibilities

    *The style and the color were all decided upon by my kids.*

    *We are still trying to decide upon a venue.*

    *He decided upon all things.*

5. **droll**  *adj.*  (old-fashioned or ironic) amusing, but not in a way that you expect

    *His story is very droll.*

He expressed a droll philosophy in his novel.

6. **angst**  *n. [U]*  (from German) a feeling of anxiety and worry about a situation, or about your life

   He loves songs full of teenage angst.

   He is full of angst about the situation.

7. **ridden**  *adj.*  (usually in compounds) full of a particular unpleasant thing

   He lived in disease-ridden slum.

   She was guilt-ridden at the way she had treated him.

   She was ridden with guilt.

8. **delude**  *v.*  to make sb believe sth that is not true

   Don't be deluded into thinking that we are out of danger yet.

   You poor deluded creature.

   He's deluding himself if he thinks it's going to be easy.

9. **garbled**  *adj.*  (of a message or story) told in a way the confuses the person listening, usually by sb who is shocked or in a hurry

   He gives a garbled account of what had happened.

   There was a garbled message from her on my answering machine.

   The teacher can't understand his garbled answer to the question.

10. **resonate**  *v. (formal)*  (of a voice, a instrument, etc.) to make a deep, clear sound that continues for a long time

    Her voice resonated through the theatre.

    The garbled voice resonated in the background.

    The room resonated with the chatter of 100 people.

11. **incomparable**  *adj.*  so good or impressive that nothing can be compared to it

    The incomparable beauty of the Lake Garda attracts many people everyday.

    Who can defeat the incomparable Frank.

    His achievements were incomparable.

12. **on the world's lips**  (sb/sth) is usually being talking about by everyone

    His incomparable achievements are on world's lips.

    Snoopy is a cartoon character on world's lips.

    He is on world's lips because of his great contributions to this country.

13. **pass away**  (also **pass on**) to die. People say "pass away" to avoid saying "die".

    His grandpa passed away yesterday.

    Most of people are very sad at his passing away.

14. **a host of**  a large number of people or things

    He has created a host of impressed icons for animations.

    He has read a host of books of biology.

15. **range from... to**  to vary between two particular amounts, sizes, etc., including others between them.

    Estimates of the damage range from $1million to $5 million.

*Accommodation ranges from tourist class to luxury hotels.*

16. **illusion** *n.* a false idea or belief, especially about sb or about a situation

    *I have no illusions about her feelings for me.*

    *She's under the illusion that she'll get the job.*

    *He could no longer distinguish between illusion and reality.*

17. **hapless** *adj.* [only before noun] (*informal*) not lucky; unfortunate

    *He was the hapless victim of exploitation.*

    *The hapless dog died yesterday.*

    *He was hapless and died in the accident.*

18. **be bent on sth / on doing sth** to be determined to do sth(usually sth bad)

    *She is bent on mastering English.*

    *He is bent on destroying the world.*

19. **wacky** *adj.* (*informal*) funny or amusing in a slightly crazy way

    *The audience was absorbed in his wacky humor.*

    *Everyone can't accept his wacky ideas.*

20. **on one's own** alone; without anyone else

    *He has fulfilled the hard task on his own.*

    *I'm all on my own today.*

    *He lives on his own.*

# Answer Keys

## I. Getting the Message

1. A   2. C   3. B   4. D   5. C

## II. Developing Your Vocabulary

### Section A

1. resonated   2. incomparable   3. fulfilled
4. animation   5. honorary   6. illusion

### Section B

1. a host of   2. passed away   3. the brains and the brawn
4. decided up   5. bent on   6. on our own

## III. Recognizing Main Ideas

1. animators   2. work on   3. cartoon   4. beagle
5. incomparable   6. spread   7. lips   8. fame

## IV. Trying the Translation

### Section A

1. 这些卡通明星使他誉满全球。
2. 一切事物都由孩子经历、评价,并最终作出决定。
3. 我实现了孩提时的抱负。
4. 他安详地去世了。
5. 他创作了一系列卡通偶像,从兔八哥到戴菲鸭到格林奇。

### Section B

1. He is a star on the world's lips.
2. He is bent on mastering English.
3. He has created a host of cartoon icons.
4. We have read a lot of works of famous writers ranging form Lu Xun, Ba Jin to Zhao shuli.
5. I fulfilled the task on my own.

## V. Organizing your ideas

f e b d c a

参考译文

# 卡通明星

**史努比的创造者:查尔斯·史库兹**

在之后将近50年的时间里,查尔斯·史库兹既是"花生"剧系列漫画的策划者也是制作者。他独自设计、研究并撰文;绘出每一副漫画,尔后刊登在世界各地的报纸上的。

尽管他深居简出,但是他绘制的这一幅幅漫画却使他名扬世界。1955和1964年他两次获得了鲁宾小金像奖,这是漫画艺术的最高荣誉。事实上,他是有史以来同时在多家报刊发表作品最多的漫画家。

对他来说,创作的唯一原则就是:一切事物都由孩子经历,评价,并最终作出决定。"这是一个童真的市场",查尔斯说,他的这一原则督促他每天去工作室"寻求"更深更广的感觉,把文笔发挥到极致,我想我已经利用自己被赋予的能力做到最好,还能要求什么呢?

查尔斯·史库兹绘画了18,250多幅"花生"系列漫画,他通过他笔下的招牌形象,包括倒霉、有深重忧虑感的Charlie Brown,浪漫而自欺欺人的小猎犬史努比、弹钢琴的Schroeder和自私自利的露西,表达了一种滑稽有趣的哲学。其中没有一个成年人,尽管偶尔有老师或父母含混不清的声音在幕后回荡。

"亲爱的朋友,在将近50年的时间里我有幸绘出了像Charlie Brown以及他的朋友们这些形象。我终于实现了我童年的抱负……"

查尔斯·史库兹的成就是无人可比的,他的作品传到75个国家,史努比也因此成了世上家喻户晓的形象。

**永远的卡通英雄：查克·琼斯**

在沃尔特·迪斯尼去世之后，查克·琼斯被动画片和电影制作者们公认为"当代动画之父"，动画界真正的领军人物。

查克·琼斯在长达60年之久的职业生涯中参加了300多部动画片制作。他制作的电影其中有三部荣获奥斯卡金像奖，从兔八哥、戴菲鸭到格林奇。

查克·琼斯认为他的卡通人物象其他东西一样是真实的。"动画不是虚幻的世界，"他在传记里说，"那是真实的生活。"

他还独自创造了一些卡通形象，最著名的有跑得飞快、嘟嘟叫的小走鸭 Road Runner 和他倒霉的追赶者——荒野狼 Wile E.Coyote。他还画了浪漫的 Pepe le Pew——一只操着法国口音的臭鼬，以及一门心思想毁灭地球的外星人 Marvin Martin。

"琼斯有时像他的卡通人物一样古怪，"他的孙子 Craig 说。他10岁时，为了动画片"白色海豹"的制作，他帮祖父研究海豹的动作。当祖父琼斯注意到海豹的骨骼结构与人类相像，于是他把孙子的踝、膝和肘分别绑在一起，换上鱼鳍，将他放到水池里，看他能否游泳。

"他看待事物与常人不同……他总是能从生活中找到快乐，找到滑稽有趣的一面，" Kausen 说。

# BARBIE DOLL'S MOM-RUTH HANDLER

## Background Information

**Ruth Handler** Since its debut in 1959, an anatomically improbable molded plastic statuette named Barbie has become an icon. Ruth Handler undeniably invented an American icon that functions as both a steady outlet for girls' dreams and an ever-changing reflection of American society. This can be seen in the history of Barbie's clothes, and even her various "face lifts" to suit the times; in her professional, political and charitable endeavors; and more recently in the multi-culturalizing of her product line.

**Her milestones**

1938 Ruth married Elliot Handler

1945 Mattel founded by Harold Matson, Elliot Handler and Ruth Handler to make picture frames

1946 Matson sells his interest to the Handlers. Mattel makes and sells doll house furniture

1959 Ruth invents a three dimension doll named Barbie

1960 The success of the Barbie doll led Mattel to become a publicly-owned company

1967 Ruth Handler becomes President of Mattel, Inc.

1974 the Handlers leave the Mattel company

## Language Points

1. **available**  *adj.*  (of things) that you can get, buy or find
   All the dolls available were made of paper and cardboard.
   He has read all the books available.
2. **dimensional**  *adj.*  having the number of dimensions mentioned
   This is a multi-dimensional model.
   Handler decided to create a three-dimensional adult female doll.
3. **executive**  *n.*  a person who has an important job as a manager of a company or an organization
   She is the executive of advertising in this company.
   He was the chief executive in a computer firm three years ago.
4. **appeal**  *n.* [U]  a quality that makes sb/sth attractive or interesting
   Her idea was rejected because they think the product has little appeal.
   The Beatles have never really lost their appeal.
   The prospect of living in a city holds little appeal for me.
5. **debut**  *v. & n.*  the first public appearance of a performer or sports player
   Barbie doll debuted at New York in 1959.
   He will make his debut for the first team this week.
6. **flag**  *v.*  to become tired, weaker or less enthusiastic
   It had been a long day and the children were beginning to flag.
   Her confidence never flagged.
7. **accessory**  *n.*  [usually] a thing that you can wear or carry that matches your clothes, for example a belt or a bag
   The hairstyle and accessories become fashion.
   Please buy some fashion accessories to dress up your wardrobe.
8. **aspiration**  *n.*  a strong desire to have or do sth
   I didn't realize that you had political aspirations.
   He has never had any aspiration to earn a lot of money.
9. **tackle**  *v.*  to make a determined effort to deal with a difficult problem or situation
   The government is determined to tackle inflation.
   I think I'll tackle the repairs next weekend.
10. **versatile**  *adj.*  (approving) (of a person) able to do many different things
    He's a versatile actor who has played a wide variety of parts.
11. **start out as (sth)**  to begin, or to begin sth such as a career, in a particular way that changed later
    It's hard to believe that Barbie doll started out as a human being.
    She started as a secretary but ended up running the whole department.
12. **swamp with (sth)**  to make sb have more of sth than they can deal with
    The company was swamped with job applications.

*Since the debut of the new product, the company was swamped with the orders.*

13. **catch up with**   to reach the same level or standard as sb who was better or more advanced

    *I'm determined to work hard to catch up with the classmate in the first place.*

    *They need to learn more knowledge to catch up with the demand of the society.*

14. **take on**   to decide to do sth; to agree to be responsible for sb/sth take of someone by helping them, giving them what they need, or keeping them safe

    *I can't take any extra work.*

    *We're not taking on any new clients at present.*

## Answer Keys

### I. Getting the Message

**Section A**

1. N    2. N    3. Y    4. N    5. N    6. NG

**Section B**

1. made of paper         2. ad executives        3. market appeal
4. New York city in 1959  5. Lili                6. millennium

### II. Recognizing main ideas

1. successful    2. behind       3. realized     4. playing with    5. instead of
6. led to        7. named after  8. released     9. instant         10. fashions

## 参考译文

### 芭比娃娃之母——露丝·汉德勒

她是成功的商业女性,摇滚乐队的成员,女子世界杯足球运动员。这个超级明星是谁?不是别人,正是芭比娃娃。很难相信她最初源于一个真人!那就是芭芭拉·汉德勒,露丝·汉德勒的女儿。

在20世纪50年代早期,露丝·汉德勒看到她的小女儿芭芭拉和她的同性小伙伴们很喜欢玩成年化的女性洋娃娃而不是小孩娃娃。汉德勒意识到让女孩子们设想她们长大后可能会变成的样子与让她们专注于将来可能会如何照顾孩子同样重要。

因为能找到的成人化洋娃娃都是用纸或纸板做的,汉德勒决定创作一个三维立体成人化洋娃娃,鲜活得足可以激发她女儿对未来梦想的灵感。汉德勒把自己的想法拿给Mattel公司的广告主管,这家公司是几年前汉德勒和她丈夫一起在她家的车库建立起来的。委员会(全男性)拒绝了她的想法,原因是成本昂贵,没有市场潜力。

这之后不久,汉德勒一次欧洲之行带回了一个叫"Lilli"的洋娃娃,这个洋娃娃是根据德国的漫画人物制成的。汉德勒花了一些时间设计了一个与"Lilli"相似的洋娃娃,而且请回了一位设计师专门为"她"量体裁衣,结果"芭比娃娃"(根据汉德勒女儿的名字取名),可爱的"邻家女孩"就诞生了。

　　Mattel公司最终同意接受汉德勒的努力,1959年芭比娃娃在纽约举行的美国玩具贸易会上首次亮相。女孩子们争相购买,芭比娃娃在第一年就为Mattel公司创造了市场销售新纪录(3美元一个,卖掉351,000个芭比娃娃)。自此,芭比娃娃热销经久不衰,直到今天,售掉足有上亿个;芭比娃娃生产线在玩具工业史上是最为成功的。

　　首例芭比娃娃梳马尾辫,穿黑白相间条纹泳装,露脚趾鞋,着太阳镜,戴耳环。这系列装束与配饰对销售也相当有效。在纽约玩具贸易年会上购买商对此印象并不深刻,但小女孩们对此却不会没有印象,这为零售商们带来了抢购热潮。Mattel公司的订单纷至沓来,足够好几年生产才能满足市场需求。

　　芭比娃娃是以一个青少年的流行模样进入市场的,但接下来的几年里她扮演了各类角色。她触及到每一个可能的职业,有牙医,医生,消防员,宇航员,古生物学家,甚至总统候选人。

　　芭比娃娃更深层地施展的多才多艺发挥她无限的作用以激发女孩们的梦想伴她们走入新千年。

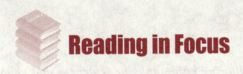

## 指代一致——英语阅读的逻辑连贯 Coherence

　　在英语语篇中所谓的指代一致是指代词与其指代的名词在性、数、格上保持一致,或者所照应的名词词组或句子在这些方面保持一致。这是英语语篇扩展,保持逻辑连贯的重要手段之一,是英语阅读应当掌握的。

| 语篇指代 | 指代模式 | 回指 | 是指被指代对象在上文中。例如:<br>Each cigarette <u>a person</u> smokes does some harm, and eventually <u>he</u> may get a serious disease for its effect. |
|---|---|---|---|
| | | 下指 | 是指被指代对象在下文中。例如:<br>I would never have believed <u>it</u>. <u>They've accepted the whole scheme.</u> |
| | 指代原则 | 就近指代 | 是指被指代对象通常在指代词前不远处,如本句或上一句或下一句中。例如:<br>"At times Jones was as wacky as his characters," said grandson <u>Craig Kausen</u>. When he was 10, <u>he</u> helped his grandfather… |
| | | 数格一致 | 被指代对象通常与指代词在数(如单数或复数)和格(主格或宾格)两方面相同。例如:<br>It was during the 1920s that the <u>friendship</u> between the two American writers reached <u>its</u> highest point. |

续表

| 语篇指代 | 指代的语篇类型 | 主从复合句中的指代 | 在主从复合句中，第二句的代词主语经常指代第一句的名词主语。例如：<br>All staff rejected the idea because they think it is too costly and has little appeal. |
|---|---|---|---|
| | | 并列动词中的指代 | 如果一个句中有两个并列的动词，第二个动词的代词宾语经常指代前一个动词后的名词宾语。例如：<br>Tom *speaks* Chinese fluently, but can't *write* in it. |
| | | 平行结构中的指代 | 平行结构主要包括 some/most/many/such/each..., others...; not only...but also...; the former...the latter 等。在这种结构中，平行结构两个部分的两个代词经常指代同一对象——前一句中的名词主语。例如：<br>Tom's view on this problem was discussed in the meeting. Most accepted it, but others rejected it. |
| | | 所有格指代 | 所有格代词经常指代其前面与其最接近的名词。例如：<br>On the way back from hiking, the girls shared their food and water to boys who had used up theirs. |

**EXERCISE**

**I. Direction: Read the following paragraphs or sentences and choose the best answer to each question.**

1. Large wind farms might also interfere with the flight patterns of migratory birds in certain areas, and they have killed large birds of prey (especially hawks, falcons, and eagles) that prefer to hunt along the same ridge lines that are ideal for wind turbines. The killing of birds of prey by wind turbines has pitted environmentalists who champion wildlife protection against environmentalists who promote renewable wind energy. Researchers are evaluating how serious this problem is and hope to find ways to eliminate or sharply reduce this problem.

   The phrase "this problem" in the passage refers to _____.

   A. interference with the flight patterns of migrating birds in certain areas

   B. building ridge lines that are ideal for wind turbines

   C. the killing of birds of prey by wind turbines

   D. meeting the demands of environmentalists who promote renewable wind energy

   本题涉及的是一个词组 this problem。寻找这一词组的指代对象时只需向上搜索就行。根据就近原则，前一句中的主语 the killing of birds of prey by wind turbines 可以初步确定为答案。将其代入原文，符合语义和逻辑，因此第三个选项为正确答案。第一个选项和第三个选项都和 this problem 相距较远，而且代入时语义和逻辑上不通，因此为干扰选项。

2. The fins are stiff, smooth, and narrow, qualities that also help cut drag. When not in use, the

fins are tucked into special grooves or depressions so that they lie flush with the body and do not break up its smooth contours.

The word "they" in the passage refers to _____.

A. qualities      B. fins      C. grooves      D. depressions

在这一例子中，从句 so that they...中的代词主语 they 指代主句的名词主语 the fins，因此第二个选项为正确答案。

3. Artists are recognizing the distinction between public and private spaces, and taking that into account when executing their public commissions.

The word "that" in line 27 refers to _____.

A. artists      B. distinction      C. public      D. private spaces

句中有两个并列的动词 recognizing 和 taking (into account)，其中 recognizing 的宾语是 distinction，而 taking 的宾语是 that。根据上述技巧，that 指代 distinction。因此，B 为正确答案。

4. In the Southwest France in the 1940s, playing children discovered Lascaux Grotto, a series of narrow cave chambers that contain huge prehistoric paintings of animals. Many of these beasts are as large as 16 feet (almost 5 meters). Some follow each other in solemn parades, but others swirl about, sideways and upside down.

The word "others" in the passage refers to _____.

A. chambers      B. paintings      C. beasts      D. parades

原文包含平行结构 some...others，它们都指代前一句中的名词主语 beasts，因此第三个选项为正确答案。

5. In many nations or countries, folk-made objects give way to their popular equivalent, usually because the popular item is more quickly or cheaply produced, is easier or time saving to use, or lends more prestige to the owner.

The word "their" in line 1 refers to _____.

A. folk      B. nations      C. countries      D. objects

根据所有格指代的解题技巧，their 指代前面位置最近的名词 objects，因此(D)为正确答案。

II. 在语篇指代中，还有一种指代的层递现象，也就是后面连续几句中的代词都同样指代第一句中的名词。请思考下面练习中的问题。

1. Jones worked on more than 300 animated films in a career that spanned more than 60 years. Three of **his** films won Academy Awards, and **he** received an honorary Oscar in 1995 for lifetime achievement. **He** has given life to a host of cartoon icons ranging from Bugs Bunny and Daffy Duck to the Grinch.

Who does **He** refer to?

根据指代的层递，文中三个黑体代词都指代前面的名词 Jones，因此 **He** 指代 Jones。

2. While such interviews can be highly entertaining, they are not necessarily an accurate indication of public opinion. First, **they** reflect the opinions of only those people who

appear at a certain location.
Who does the second **they** refer to?

　　在这一例子中,第二句中的代词 they (reflect the opinions...) 对应第一句中的 they (are not...),而第一个 they 指代前面从句中的名词主语 interviews,那么第二个 they 也指代 interviews.

# Unit Eleven

# Power of Music

## Script for Lead-in Listening

Listen to the following conversation and fill in the blanks with the correct words or phrases. You may choose the words or phrases from the list given.

Alice:     I heard that Ben is forming his own band.
Jack:     It will probably be a rock and roll band. He's a very good guitarist.
Alice:     Can you play a musical instrument? If you can, he might ask you to join the band.
Jack:     I can play the drums, but I haven't played for a while. I'm not sure I'd be good enough to play in a band.
Alice:     I wish I could play a musical instrument. I love music.
Jack:     Nowadays, you can be a DJ. You can mix dance music. It doesn't take a lot of practice.
Alice:     You know, you could probably get a computer program that would help you. You already have a computer, so you could use that to help you mix some music.
Jack:     That's a great idea. I'll search for some information on the internet. If it's possible to do, the internet will have some information about it.

## WORDS AND PHRASES IN LEAD-IN LISTENING

**nowadays** *adj.* at the present time, in contrast with the past
*Nowadays most kids prefer watching TV to reading.*

**mix** *v.* *(technical)* to combine different recordings of voices and/or instruments to produce a single piece of music

**search for (sb/sth)** *(computing)* an act of looking for information in a computer database or network.

# TEXT A

## KEEP ON SINGING

 ### Background Information

1. **Intensive Care Unit (ICU)**  An intensive care unit (ICU), critical care unit (CCU), intensive therapy unit or intensive treatment unit (ITU) is a specialized department in a hospital that provides intensive care medicine. Many hospitals also have designated intensive care areas for certain specialties of medicine, as dictated by the needs and available resources of each hospital. The naming is not rigidly standardized.

2. **Neonatal Intensive Care Unit (NICU)**  Usually shortened NICU (pronounced "Nicky-oo") and also called a newborn intensive care unit, intensive care nursery (ICN), and special care baby unit (SCBU, pronounced "Skiboo"), especially in Great Britain), is a unit of a hospital specializing in the care of ill or premature newborn infants. The NICU is distinct from the special care nursery (SCN) in providing a high level of intensive care to premature infants while the SCN provides specialized care for infants with less severe medical problems.

   NICUs were developed in the 1950s and 1960s by pediatricians to provide better temperature support, isolation from infection risk, specialized feeding, and access to specialized equipment and resources. Infants are cared for in incubators or "open warmers." Some low birth weight infants need respiratory support ranging from extra oxygen (by head hood or nasal cannula) to continuous positive airway pressure (CPAP) or mechanical ventilation. Public access is limited, and staff and visitors are required to take precautions to reduce transmission of infection. Nearly all children's hospitals have NICUs, but they can be found in large general hospitals as well.

   A NICU is typically directed by one or more neonatologists and staffed by nurses, nurse practitioners, physician assistants, resident physicians, and respiratory therapists. Many other ancillary services are necessary for a top-level NICU. Other physicians, especially those with "organ-defined" specialties often assist in the care of these infants.

 ### Language Points

1. **tummy**  *n. (informal)*  (used especially by children or when speaking to children) the stomach or the area around the stomach

   *Mum, my tummy hurts.*
   have (a) tummy ache
   a tummy bug/upset (=an illness when you feel sick or vomit)

2. **pregnancy**  *n.* [U, C]  the state of being pregnant
    a pregnancy test
    unplanned/unwanted pregnancies
    the increase in teenage pregnancies

    **pregnant**  *adj.* (of a women or female animal) having a baby or young animal developing inside her/its body
    She was pregnant with her third child at the time.
    get/become pregnant
    She's six months pregnant.

3. **labor**  *n.* [U,C, usually sing.]  the period of time or the process of giving birth to a baby
    Jane was in labor for ten hours.
    She went into labor early.

4. **siren**  *n.*  a device that makes a long loud sound as a signal or warning
    an air-raid siren
    A police car raced past with its siren wailing.

5. **howl**  *v.*  to make a long, loud noise
    The wind was howling around the house.
    he crowd howled their displeasure.

6. **inch**  *v.*  to move or make sth move slowly and carefully in a particular direction
    inch one's way forward
    inch along a ledge on a cliff
    I inched the car forward.

7. **be prepared for**  ready and able to deal with sth
    be prepared for anything to happen
    be prepared for power cuts by buying a lot of candles.

8. **burial**  *n.* [U, C]  the act or ceremony of burying a dead body
    a burial place/mound/site
    Her body was sent home for burial.

9. **fix up**  to repair, decorate or make sth ready
    *fix up the motor*
    *fix up a meeting with sb*
    You have to fix visits up in advance with the museum.

10. **funeral**  *n.*  a ceremony, usually a religious one, for burying a dead person
    a funeral procession
    a funeral march
    Hundreds of people attended the funeral.

11. **as if /as though**  in a way that suggests sth
    It sounds as if you had a good time.
    It's my birthday. As if you didn't know!
    He treats me as if I were a stranger.

12. **alive**　*adj.*　[not before noun] living; not dead

    Is your mother still alive?

    She had to steal food just to stay alive.

    He was buried alive in the earthquake.

13. **scrub**　*n.* [sing.]　an act of cleaning sth by rubbing it hard

    I've given the floor a good scrub.

14. **laundry**　*n.* [U]　clothes, sheets, etc. that need washing, that are being washed, or that have been washed recently

    a pile of clean/dirty/laundry

    a laundry basket/room

15. **mild**　*adj.*　(of people or their behaviour) gentle and kind; not usually getting angry or violent

    a mild woman, who never shouted

    **mildly**　*adv.*　in a gentle manner

    "I didn't mean to upset you," he said mildly.

16. **firmly**　*adv.*　in a strong or definite way

    "I can manage," she said firmly.

    **firm**　*adj.*　not easily changed or influenced; showing strength of character and purpose

    a firm faith

    a firm believer in socialism

17. **pure**　*adj.*　[usually before noun] not mixed with anything else; with nothing added

    pure gold/silk

    These shirts are 100% pure cotton.

    One movie is classified as pure art, the other as entertainment.

    **purity**　*n.* [U]　the state or quality of being pure

    moral/spiritual purity

18. **steady**　*adj.*　not changing and not interrupted

    She drove at a steady 50 mph.

    a steady boyfriend/girlfriend

    have a steady relationship

19. **healing**　*n.*　the process of becoming or making sb/sth healthy again; the process of getting better after an emotional shock

    the healing process

    emotional healing

20. **sweep**　*v.*　to suddenly affect sb strongly

    A wave of tiredness swept over her.

    Memories came sweeping back.

21. **cancel**　*v.*　to decide that sth that has been arranged will not now take place

    The sports meeting was cancelled.

    Don't forget to cancel the newspaper (=arrange for it not to be delivered) before going away.

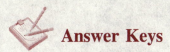

# Answer Keys

## I. Getting the Message
1. B    2. D    3. C    4. B    5. D

## II. Developing Your Vocabulary
### Section A
1. inching    2. firmly    3. purity    4. steady    5. prepared    6. pregnancy

### Section B
1. on the way    2. canceled    3. alive    4. strained    5. dress...in    6. as if

## III. Recognizing Main Ideas
1. pregnant    2. sing    3. unfortunately    4. condition
5. for    6. allowed to    7. again    8. health

## IV. Trying the Translation
### Section A
1. 他一点一点地穿过狭窄的通道。
2. 她又怀孕了。
3. 他的家人坚持应该为他举行像样的葬礼。
4. 现在它已稳稳地确立为国内主要品牌之一。
5. 他表现得若无其事。

### Section B
1. They fixed up the house before they moved in.
2. Doctor kept the baby alive for six weeks.
3. He cancelled his order for the goods.
4. She dressed herself and the children in their best clothes.
5. He spoke in a low, strained voice.

## V. Organizing your ideas
d    a    f    e    c    b

## 参考译文

### 别放弃歌唱

像其他的好妈妈一样,当卡伦发现自己又怀孕了时,她就尽力帮她三岁的儿子迈克尔做好准备迎接这个新生儿的到来。他们知道了这是个女孩,于是,日复一日,一夜又一夜,迈克尔趴在妈妈肚子上为他的小妹妹唱歌。

卡伦的怀孕期进展正常。接着产前阵痛就来临了。每5分钟一次……每分钟一次。阵痛持续了几个小时。终于,迈克尔的小妹妹降生了。但她的情况很严重。伴着警报器的鸣叫声,救护车把婴儿送到田纳西州诺克斯维尔市的圣玛丽医院。

日子一天天过去了,女婴的情况愈来愈糟。小儿科专家告诉这对父母:"希望非常渺茫。请做好最坏的打算吧。"卡伦和她的丈夫联系了当地一家公墓。他们在家里布置好了一间特别的婴儿房——现在却要计划一个葬礼。

迈克尔一直乞求父母让他进去看看小妹妹:"我想唱歌给她听,"他说。这是重症特护的第二周了。看来好像到不了这周结束葬礼就要来临了。迈克尔不断地缠着要给小妹妹唱歌听,然而重症特护区不允许儿童入内。不过卡伦下定了决心,不管他们愿不愿意,她都要带迈克尔进去。如果现在他看不到他的小妹妹,就再也没机会见到她了。

她为儿子穿了一身特大型的洗刷服,带他走进重症监护室。他看起来就像一个行走的洗衣篮,不过护士长认出这是一个孩子,她吼道:"马上带那个孩子离开这儿!禁止小孩入内。"卡伦的母性变得坚强起来,这位平日里温柔的女士用坚毅的目光盯着护士长的脸,坚定地说:"他不会离开的,除非给他妹妹唱首歌。"卡伦拉着迈克尔走到他小妹妹的床前。他盯着这个不再为生存而挣扎的小婴儿,开始唱歌。用三岁孩子单纯的心声,迈克尔唱道:

"你是我的阳光,唯一的阳光,当天空灰暗你能使我快乐——"女婴立刻有了反应。脉搏跳动变得平静而稳定。

迈克尔一直在唱着:"亲爱的,你从来不知道我有多么爱你。请不要带走我的阳光——"紧张的呼吸变得那般安稳。

迈克尔继续唱着:"亲爱的,那天晚上当我睡着,我梦到我把你抱在怀中……"他的小妹妹仿佛在休息般地放松下来了,康复般的休息似乎在她身上扩展开来。迈克尔还在唱着。泪水在护士长的脸上肆意流着。"你是我的阳光,唯一的阳光。请别带走我的阳光。"

葬礼计划取消了。第二天——就在第二天——女婴就好起来,可以回家了!

# TEXT B

# MUSIC HAS POWER

## Background Information

**Harvey Reid**   A musician living in Maine.   And he is quite possibly the best acoustic guitarist you've never heard of.   His credits include winning the 1981 National Fingerpicking Guitar Competition, once winning the Beanblossom bluegrass guitar contest. His Steel Drivin' Man CD was voted in 1996 by Acoustic Guitar Magazine as one of the 10 Essential Folk CD's of all time. A multi-instrumentalist,   Harvey was also the 1982 International Autoharp Champion,   plays the six-string banjo, mandolin and bouzouki.

  Songwriter and multi-instrumentalist Harvey Reid has honed his craft over the last 33 years in countless clubs, festivals, street corners, cafes, schools and concert halls across the nation. He has been called a "giant of the steel strings" and "one of the true treasures of American acoustic music." He has absorbed a vast repertoire of American contemporary and roots music and woven it into his own colorful, personal and distinctive style. His 20 recordings on Woodpecker Records showcase his mastery of many instruments and styles of acoustic music,   from hip folk to slashing slide guitar blues to bluegrass, old-time, Celtic, ragtime, and even classical.

## Language Points

1. **rhythm**   *n.* [U,C]   a strong regular repeated pattern of sounds or movements
     *The boat rocked up and down in rhythm with the sea.*
     *The rhythm of her breathing*
     *a dancer with a natural sense of rhythm (=the ability to move in time to fixed beat)*
2. **involve**   *v.*   if a situation, an event or an activity involves sth, that thing is an important or necessary part of it
     *Any investment involves an element of risk.*
     *Many of the crimes involved drugs.*
     *The test will involve answering questions about a photograph.*
   **involved**   *adj.*   [not usually before noun] giving a lot of time or attention to sb/sth
     *She was deeply involved with the local hospital.*
     *I was so involved in my book I didn't hear you knock.*
     *He's a very involved father (=he spends a lot of time with his children).*
3. **offer**   *v.*   to say that you are willing to do sth for sb or give sth to sb
     *He offered $ 4,000 for the car.*
     *Josie had offered her services as a guide.*
     *He offered some useful advice.*

4. **skilled**  adj.  having enough ability, experience and knowledge to be able to do sth well

    a skilled engineer/negotiator/ craftsman

    She is highly skilled at dealing with difficult customers.

    a shortage of skilled labour(=people who have had training in a skill)

5. **profound**  adj.  needing a lot of study or thought

    profound questions about life and death

    a profound theory

    profound mysteries

6. **only**  adv.  in formal written English only, or only if and its clause, can be placed first in the sentence. In the second part of the sentence, be, do, have, etc. come before the subject and the main part of the verb.

    Only in Paris do you find bars like this.

    Only if these conditions are fulfilled can the application proceed to the next stage.

    Only then did she realize the stress he was under.

7. **aspect**  n. [C]  a particular part or feature of a situation, an idea, a problem, etc.

    The book aims to cover all aspects of city life.

    She felt she had looked at the problem from every aspect.

    This was one aspect of her character he hadn't seen before.

8. **awareness**  n.  knowing sth; knowing that sth exists and is important

    awareness of the importance of eating a healthy diet

    There was an almost complete lack of awareness of the issues involved.

    It is important that students develop an awareness of how the Internet can be used.

9. **various**  adj.  several different

    Tents come in various shapes and sizes.

    She took the job for various reasons.

    There are various ways of doing this.

    **variously**  adv. (written) in servenl different ways

        He has been variously described as a hero, a genius and a bully.

        The cost has been variously estimated at between $10 million and $20 million.

    **variety**  n. [sing.]  several different sorts of the same thing.

        He resigned for a variety of reasons.

        There is a wide variety of patterns to choose from.

10. **progress**  v.  to improve or develop over a period of time

    The course allows students to progress at their own speed.

    Work on the new road is progressing slowly.

11. **mastery**  n. [U, sing.]  having knowledge about or understanding of a particular thing

    She has mastery of several languages.

    His mastery of the violin

12. **set out**  to leave a place and begin a journey

    They set out on the last stage of their journey.

*They set out at dawn.*
*He set out with the best intentions.*

**set out to do sth** to begin a job, task, etc. with a particular aim or goal
*He set out to break the world record.*
*They succeeded in what they set out to do.*

13. **essential** *adj.* completely necessary; extremely important in a particular situation or for a particular activity
*an essential part/ingredient/component of something*
*Money is not essential to happiness.*
*It is essential to keep the two groups separate.*

14. **sacred** *adj.* connected with God or a god; considered to be holy
*a sacred image/shrine/temple*
*sacred music*
*Cows are sacred to Hindus.*

15. **inaccessible** *adj.* difficult or impossible to reach or to get
*Dirt can collect in inaccessible places.*
*The temple is now inaccessible to the public.*
*The language of teenagers is often completely inaccessible to (=not understood by) adults.*

16. **joyous** *adj. (literary)* very happy; causing people to be happy
    **joyful** *adj. (written)* very happy; causing people to be happy
*She gave a joyful laugh.*
*It was a joyful reunion of all the family.*
    **joyless** *adj. (written)* bringing no happiness; without joy
*a joyless marriage/childhood*

17. **unfold** *v.* to spread open or flat sth that has previously been folded; to become open and flat
*to unfold a map/tablecloth/letter*
*She unfolded her arms.*

18. **other than** *(written)* different or differently from; not
*The truth is quite other than what you think.*
*I have never known him to behave other than selfishly.*

19. **relatively** *adv.* to a fairly large degree, especially in comparison to others
*I found the test relatively easy.*
*We had relatively few applications for the job.*
*Lack of exercise is also a risk factor for heart disease but it's relatively small when compared with others.*

    **relatively speaking** used when you are comparing sth with all similar things

20. **constant** *adj.* [usually before noun] happening all the time or repeatedly
*constant interruptions*
*a constant stream of visitors all day*
*Babies need constant attention.*

**constantly** *adv.* all the time; repeatedly
Fashion is constantly changing.
Heat the sauce, stirring constantly.

21. **if not** used to introduce a different suggestion, after a sentence with if
I'll go if you're going. If not (= if you are not) I'd rather stay at home.
Go to bed. If not, I'll tell mother.

# Answer Keys

## I. Getting the Message
### Section A
1. Y  2. Y  3. N  4. Y  5. N  6. NG

### Section B
1. involved in music  2. thoughts and feelings  3. voice do
4. aspects of the art  5. inside us  6. go further

## II. Recognizing main ideas
1. place  2. not only  3. skilled  4. essential  5. love
6. appreciation  7. part  8. involves  9. experience  10. control

## 音乐有力量

吉他音乐是多元素交汇的集合体,里面包含了节奏、音调、情感、和谐、诗意、准备、友谊、智慧、体力的训练和灵魂的修养。它涉及了你的精神、你的肉体、你的心灵和你的情绪,它是既自我又公开的行为。它不单给演奏者以创作音乐的愉悦感,也让那些技巧娴熟的人得以通过音乐影响他人的思想和感受。通过演奏你喜爱的吉他,你可以让人明白深奥的道理,并懂得珍惜。

只有当你倾注一生去热爱音乐,你才有可能体验到音乐方方面面的魅力。而对音乐多元素的基本了解和经常性的体验,能大大加快学生对音乐的领悟和掌握。而要达到这个目标就要付出艰辛的代价,要拥有影响他人思想和感受的能力,你必须承担相应的责任,也并不是所有学音乐的人都能坚持到最后。

音乐学习的精髓在于对音乐的热忱,和对音乐的膜拜。音乐并不是由你的手,或是你的声音可以制造出来的,有时甚至也不是你的灵感创造出来的。音乐的最佳境界是种超出人类体验的境界,它囊括了你的灵与肉,让你得以存在于波浪的顶尖,当你演绎每部分音乐的时候,你的身心已与你演绎的音乐密不可分。只有到了这个境界,我们才能算真正地活在人世上,才算真正意义上的掌控自己的命运,因为在那个时刻,我们没有了过去,也没有了将来。

当你沉浸在音乐当中,当你娴熟地运用音乐,你可以体验到那种不可替代的愉悦感。音乐创造所带来的愉悦感是所有学音乐的人孜孜以求的目标。如果音乐创作的时间足够长,与人分享美妙音乐的意愿足够强烈和真诚,你的双手、你的嗓音都会自觉地做出相应的调整,演绎最真实的你。你不能催生这个过程,你只需要耐心的体验其中的每一个细节。以后当你回忆起自己音乐生涯的起步经历,你就会明白初学者享受到的无拘无束的自由。对自己过高的要求会束缚你的成长,因为音乐带给人们的愉悦感是相对稳定的,如果你在做学生的时候都体会不到这种愉悦感和满足感,那在你继续深造以前,你必须更加努力。音乐的神奇之处在于它是源自我们的内心,初学者可以和音乐大师们一样轻松地体验到其中的魅力,说不定更加容易。

## Reading in Focus

英语句子中的省略 What Is Missing?

## EXERCISE

*I. Direction: Read the following sentences carefully. Cross the unnecessary words with a slash "/".*

1. Her job is to take care of the elders and (to) wash their clothes.
2. You can play the game just as wonderfully as I (do).
3. I guess Lisa will dance in the party but Jane won't (dance in the party).
4. Her parents don't know when (she was born) and where she was born.
5. John won the first race and Jimmy (won) the second (race).
6. The captain can find a boat quicker than we can (find a boat).
7. Doctors have said that as many as 50% of patients don't take medicine as (it is) directed.
8. Tom was attacked by cramp while (he was) swimming across the river.
9. Someone traveling alone, if (he is) hungry, injured, or ill, often had nowhere to turn except to the nearest cabin or settlement.
10. This is a fine hall you have here. I've never lectured in a finer (hall).

# Unit Twelve

## Fans Forever

 ### Script for Lead-in Listening

Listen to the following conversation and fill in the blanks with the correct words or phrases. See how to express one's attitudes towards something or somebody.

**Ruth:** What's your favorite ball sport?
**Brian:** I like basketball. I really enjoy watching NBA games on TV.
**Ruth:** Who's your favorite player?
**Brian:** I don't really have one, but I support Houston.
**Ruth:** Do they have a good team?
**Brian:** I think they do, but I'm biased. They have a good manager and a great coach.
**Ruth:** I can't keep up with the game. The players are so fast that I can hardly see what they're doing.
**Brian:** I have the same problem. The players are really very skilful. I wish I could play that well.
**Ruth:** You play for an amateur team, don't you?
**Brian:** Yes, I do. We're doing pretty well this season. We've won most of our games, but we're not top in the league table.
**Ruth:** How many more games are there this season?
**Brian:** We've got four more games. I hope we can win all of them.

### WORDS AND EXPRESSIONS IN LEAD-IN LISTENING

**favorite** *adj.* like more than others of the same kind
  *It's one of my favorite movies.*
**biased** *adj.* making unfair judgements
  *a biased jury*
**amateur** *adj.* [usually before noun] doing sth for enjoyment
  *an enthusiastic amateur photographer*
**season** *n.* a period of time during a year when a particular activity happens
**league** *n.* a group of sports team who all play each other to earn points and find which team is best
**post** *n.* goalpost
**tackle** *v.* (in football, hockey) to try and take the ball from the opponent

# TEXT A

## WORLD CUP DAD

### Background Information

**The 2002 FIFA World Cup**  The 17th staging of the World Cup, was held in South Korea and Japan from May 31 to June 30. The two countries were chosen as hosts by FIFA in May 1996. For the first time in its history, the World Cup was organized by two countries. It was also the first World Cup held in Asia. Brazil won the tournament for a record fifth time, beating Germany 2-0 in the final.

### Language Points

1. **action**  *n.*  the process of doing sth in order to make it happen or to deal with a situation; a thing that sb does
   *Firefighters took action immediately to stop the blaze spreading.*
   *She began to explain her plan of action to the group.*
   *Her quick action saved the child's life.*

2. **get used to sth/to doing sth**  familiar with sth because you do it or experience it often
   *I am not used to eating so much at lunchtime.*
   *I found the job tiring at first but I soon got used to it.*

3. **talkative**  *adj.*  liking to talk a lot
   *He is not very talkative, except on the subject of his plants.*
   *She was in a talkative mood.*

4. **take a few days off**  to have a period of time as a break from the work
   *I have decided to take a few days off next week.*
   *I have to take a few days off to finish my paper.*

5. **reserve**  *v.*  to ask for a seat, table, room, ect. to be available for you at a future time; to keep sth for sb
   *I'd like to reserve a table for three for eight o'clock.*
   *I've reserved a room in the name of Jones.*
   *These seats are reserved for special guests.*

   **reserved**  *adj.*  (of a person or their character) slow or unwilling to show feelings or express opinions
   *a reserved man/manner*
   *He is reversed, seldom showinghis thoughts.*

6. **jabber**  *v.*  to talk quickly and in an excited way so that it is difficult to understand what you are saying

   What is he jabbering about now?

   They are jabbering away in French.

7. **figure sb/sth out**  to think about sb/sth until understand it/them; to calculate an amount or the cost of sth

   We have never been able to figure her out.

   I can't figure out how to do this.

   Have you figured out how much the trip will cost?

8. **chase**  *v.*  to run, drive, after sb/sth in order to catch them

   My dog likes chasing rabbits.

   The kids chased each other around the kitchen table.

   He chased after the burglar but couldn't catch him.

9. **silly**  *adj.*  showing a lack of thought, understanding or judgement

   That was a silly thing to do!

   Her work is full of silly mistakes.

   "I can walk home."——"Don't be silly, its much too far! "

10. **curious**  *adj.*  having a strong desire to know about sth

    They were very curious about the people who lived upstairs.

    I was curious to find out what she had said.

    He is such a curious boy, always asking questions.

11. **combine**  *v.*  to come together or to form a single thing or group

    Hydrogen and oxygen combine to form water.

    Several factors had combined to ruin our plan.

    Combine the eggs with a little flour and heat the mixture gently.

12. **remark**  *v.*  to say or write a comment about sth/sb

    She remarked how tired I was looking.

    "It's much cold than yesterday," he remarked casually.

    Critics remarked that the play was not original.

13. **transfix**  *v.*  [usually passive] to be unable to move because sth has all your attention, or because you are afraid, surprised, etc.

    Lusia stood transfixed with shock.

14. **stare at sb/sth**  to look at sb/sth for a long time

    I screamed and everyone stared.

    I stared blankly at the paper in front of me.

    He sat staring into space.

15. **bored**  *adj.*  feeling tired and impatient because you have lost interest in sb/sth or because you have nothing to do

    The children quickly got bored with staying indoors.

*There was a bored expression on her face.*

16. **lure**  *v.*  to persuade or trick sb to go somewhere or to do sth by promising them a reward
    *The child was lured into a car but managed to escape.*
    *Yong people are lured to the city by the prospect of a job and money.*
    *Few can resist the lure of adventure.*

17. **roar**  *v.*  to make a very loud, deep sound
    *We heard a lion roar.*
    *The engine roared to life.*
    *The wind was roaring in my eyes.*

18. **score**  *v.*  to win points, goals, etc. in a game or competition
    *Fraser scored again in the second half.*
    *score a goal*

19. **amaze**  *v.*  to surprise sb very much
    *Just the size of the place amazed her.*
    *It never ceases to amaze me what some people will do for money.*

    **amazed**  *adj.*  very surprised
    *an amazed silence*
    *I was amazed at her knowledge of French literature.*
    *We were amazed by his generosity.*

20. **absorb**  *v.*  to interest sb very much so that they pay no attention to anything else
    *This work had absorbed him for several years.*
    *Black walls absorb a lot of heat during the day.*
    *Plants absorb oxygen.*

21. **fight sb/sth off**  to resist sb/sth by fighting against them/it
    *The jeweller was stabbed as he tried to fight the robbers off.*
    *They united to fight off invaders.*

22. **assure**  *v.*  to tell sb that sth is definitely true or is definitely going to happen
    *I know you think I did it deliberately, but I assure you that I did not.*
    *We were assured that everything possible was being done.*
    *She is perfectly safe, I assure you.*

23. **now that**  because the thing mentioned is happening or has just happened
    *Now that the kids have left home we've got a lot of extra space.*
    *Now that they have taken matters into their hands, the pace of events has quickened.*

24. **not see eye to eye with sb (on sth)**  not to share the same views as sb about sth

25. **predict**  *v.*  to say that sth will happen in the future
    *Nobody would predict the outcome.*
    *It is impossible to predict what will happen.*
    *She predicted that the election result would be close.*

26. **triumph** *v.* to defeat sb/sth
    As is used in this kind of movie, good triumphs over evil in the end.
    France triumphed 3-0 in the final.

27. **defend** *v.* to protect sb/sth from attack
    All our officers are trained to defend themselves against knife attacks.
    It is impossible to defend against an all-out attack.
    Troops have been sent to defend the borders.

28. **concede** *v.* to admit sth is true, logical, etc.
    He was forced to concede that there might be difficulties.
    I had to concede the logic of this.
    He reluctantly conceded the point to me.

29. **foster** *v.* to encourage sth to develop
    The club's aim is to foster better relations with the community.
    They did this to foster spirit of cooperation.

# Answer Keys

## I. Getting the Message
1. C    2. A    3. A    4. C    5. A

## II. Developing Your Vocabulary
### Section A
1. interrupting  2. talkative  3. jabbering  4. absorbed  5. triumph  6. conceded

### Section B
1. came to         2. say hello        3. was traded to       4. outside of
5. paraded by and shook hands          6. between fans and their heroes

## III. Recognizing Main Ideas
1. talkative    2. hard       3. behaved     4. curiosity
5. soccer       6. in detail  7. pleasure    8. communicate

## IV. Trying the Translation
### Section A
1. 他们对住在楼上的人感到很好奇。
2. 几种因素加在一起毁了我们的计划。
3. 他好像更多的是在用行动来表达自己的爱,而不是语言。
4. 我对足球从来都不感兴趣,总觉得那就是 22 个老爷们傻乎乎地追着一颗球跑来跑去的游戏。可是,老爸这样激动让我感到很好奇。

5. 明白了比赛规则,世界杯比赛一下子变得有趣了。

**Section B**

1. I'd like to reserve a table for three for eight o'clock.
2. We have never been able to figure her out..
3. There was a bored expression on her face.
4. Fraser scored again in the second half.
5. Troops have been sent to defend the borders.

**V. Organizing Your Ideas**

d a b f c e

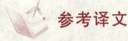
参考译文

## 世界杯老爸

老爸不善言谈,直到有一天我终于走进了他那沉默的世界。

在我15年成长的大部分时间里,老爸通常很少跟我和妈妈说话,和他交谈很困难,他好像更多的是在用行动来表达自己的爱,而不是语言。所以我也不得不接受并适应了这一事实。

但是2002年5月31日那天,一切都改变了。那天,老爸突然请了几天假来陪我和妈妈。

早上从楼上下来,我便感觉到老爸不像平时那么沉默。"世界杯!我简直等不及了!"他一直这样叫嚷着:"这么大的比赛,一定要看!"很快,我便意识到了他这么兴奋的原因:老爸是个超级足球迷,世界杯锦标赛就要开始了。

我对足球从来都不感兴趣,总觉得那就是22个老爷们傻乎乎地追着一颗球跑来跑去的游戏。可是,老爸这样激动让我感到很好奇。

当天晚上,爸爸决定带我们去一家德国饭店吃饭。那家饭店将会转播法国队对塞内加尔队的比赛。这样的话,晚上我们便可以既待在外面又能够看上世界杯了。

进店不久,比赛就开始了。老爸笑着说:"我们来的正是时候!"他目不转睛地注视着电视屏幕上那片绿茵场地,紧紧盯着那群跑来跑去的球员。我无聊地扫视着整个饭店,真不知道当初自己怎么就被他给引诱来了。

我正吃香肠的时候,突然听见电视里一阵喧哗。"迪奥普进球了!"老爸解释道。

我看着电视屏幕问道:"那个人为什么来来回回老跳呢?"

老爸耐心地解释道:"那个就是迪奥普,球员进球后都会这样,尤其赛前不被看好的时候。"

我还是有点奇怪,老爸便耐心地一一解释给我听。那个不多说话的老爸突然成了过去,而我更喜欢现在的老爸。

我开始看剩下的比赛,并且越看越投入。看着塞内加尔队一点一点地击败法国队,真的难以相信他们赛前并不被看好。为了让我看得更明白,老爸接着又给我讲了一些足球比赛的规则。也就是从那天晚上起,我的词典里开始有了诸如任意球、左后卫、犯规、罚球、越位等足球比赛的词汇。

明白了比赛规则,世界杯比赛一下子变得有趣了。接下来,我陪老爸一起看了四分之一赛、半决赛及决赛。有时候,我们意见不一致,我预测巴西队会赢得世界杯,老爸却坚持认为德国队会最终得胜,理由是他们拥有世界级的守门员卡恩。当巴西队最后捧得冠军时,老爸低下头,不情愿却又装作很大度地说:"看来我这个一级足球私人教练教得不错嘛!"我们都笑了。

足球确实拉近了老爸和我的距离,并且使我们的关系更加紧密。是谁说足球不过是22个老爷们傻乎乎地追着一颗球跑来着?

# TEXT B

# ROGER MARIS AND ME

## Background Information

1. **Roger Eugene Maris** (September 10, 1934—December 14, 1985) An American right fielder in Major League Baseball who is primarily remembered for breaking Babe Ruth's single-season home run record in 1961, a record that would stand for 37 years. In twelve Major League seasons, he participated in seven World Series.

2. **New York Yankees** A professional baseball team based in the borough of the Bronx, in New York City, New York. The Yankees are a member of the Eastern Division of Major League Baseball's American League. One of the American League's eight charter franchises, the club was founded in Baltimore, Maryland in 1901 as the Baltimore Orioles, moved to New York City in 1903, then becoming known as the New York Highlanders, and became solely known as the "Yankees" in 1913. From 1923 to the present, the Yankees permanent home has been Yankee Stadium. In 2009, they are scheduled to move into a new stadium, also to be called "Yankee Stadium".

   The Yankees have been Major League Baseball's most successful franchise with 26 World Series championships and 39 American League Pennants. They have also won the most titles of any North American franchise in professional sports history, passing the Montreal Canadiens' 24 in 1999.

3. **St. Louis Cardinals** (also referred to as "the Cards" or "the Redbirds") A professional baseball team based in St. Louis, Missouri. They are members of the Central Division in the National League of Major League Baseball. The Cardinals have won a National League record 10 World Series championships, second only to the New York Yankees in Major League Baseball who have 26.

   The Cardinals were founded in the American Association in 1882 as the St. Louis Brown Stockings, taking the name from an earlier National League team. They joined the National League in 1892 and have been known as the Cardinals since 1900. The Cardinals began play in the current Busch Stadium in 2006, becoming the first team since 1923 to win the World Series in their first season in a new ballpark. The Cardinals have a strong rivalry with the Chicago Cubs that began in 1885

## Language Points

1. **headline**  *n.*  the title of a newspaper article printed in large letters, especially at the top of the front page

   They ran the story under the headline "Home at last".

   The scandal was in the headlines for several days.

2. **rejuvenate**  *v.*  to make sb/sth look or feel younger or more lively

   His new job seemed to rejuvenate him.

   Special creams to rejuvenate the skin.

3. **swing**  *v.*  to try to hit sb/sth

   She swung at me with the iron bar.

   He swung another punch in my direction.

4. **bat**  *n.*  a piece of wood with a handle, made in various shapes and sizes, and used for hitting the ball in games such as baseball, cricket and table tennis

   *v.*  to hit a ball with a bat, especially in a game of baseball or cricket

   He bats very well.

   Who's batting first for the Orioles?

5. **stun**  *v.*  to surprise or shock sb so much that they cannot think clearly or speak

   Her words stunned me—I had no idea she felt that way.

   There was a stunned silence when I told them the news.

6. **trade**  *v.*  to buy and sell things

   Early explorers traded directly with the Indians.

   Our products are now traded worldwide.

7. **go off**  to leave a place, especially in order to do sth

   She went off to get a drink.

   The boy went off to meet his father.

8. **setting**  *n.*  a set of surroundings; the place at which sth happens

   It was a perfect setting for a wonderful Christmas.

   People tend to behave differently in different social settings.

9. **quaver**  *v.*  if sb's voice quavers, it is unsteady, usually because the person is nervous or afraid

   "I am not safe here, am I?" she asked in a quavering voice.

   She was quavering inwardly with neverousness.

10. **parade**  *v.*  to walk somewhere in a formal group of people, in order to celebrate or protest about sth; to show sb/sth in public; to come together

    The victorious team will parade through the city tomorrow morning.

    The crowds applauded as the guards paraded past.

11. **autograph**  *v.*  to sigh your name on sth for sb to keep

    The whole team has autographed a football, which will be used as a prize.

    The star autographed the picture for the boy.

12. **hold**  *v.*  to have a belief or an opinion about sb/sth

    He holds strange views on education.

    She is held in high regard by her students.

13. **mystical**  *adj.*  having spiritual powers or qualities that are difficult to understand or to explain

    Watching the sun rise over the mountain was an almost mystical experience.

    They call it the mystical rose.

14. **back**  *v.*  to move or make sth move backwards

    He backed against the wall, terrified.

    If you can't drive in forwards, try backing it in.

15. **amazing**  *adj.*  very surprising

    That's amazing, isn't it?

    It's amazing how quickly people adapt.

16. **remote**  *adj.*  far away from places where other people live; far away in time

    The farmhouse is remote from any other buildings.

    in the remote past / future

17. **magic**  *adj.*  having or using special powers to make impossible things happen or seem to happen

    a magic spell

    There is no magic formula for passing exams-only hard work.

# Answer Keys

## I. Getting the Message

### Section A

1. Y    2. N    3. NG    4. NG    5. Y    6. N

### Section B

1. by Roger Maris             2. what a big fan I was
3. was traded to the St. Louise Cardinals    4. Yankee Stadium
5. paraded by and shook hands    6. fans and their heroes

## II. Recognizing Main Ideas

1. fan     2. attracted    3. match    4. traded    5. sad
6. drove   7. outside      8. hit      9. explain   10. seldom

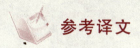

参考译文

## 罗杰·马里斯和我

我在洋基球场长大,并且喜欢上了棒球。

我11岁那年,罗杰·马里斯来到新纽约洋基队打球。记得当时有个报纸头条上写着"罗杰·马里斯为洋基队注入新血液",以前我从来没有听说过这样的话,但从中我能够感觉到,罗杰·马里斯一定不是个普通的人物。

对我来说,他挥棒的姿势,打右场的样子以及他的长相都是那么特别。我常常坐在右场31区162-A排1号座上,每次都会提前两个小时到达球场,看着他停好车,跟他打招呼,然后再告诉他我是他的超级球迷。不久,他便开始注意我了。

1966年12月8日,马里斯转会到了圣路易斯红雀棒球队,这天对我来说是个伤心日。就在那一年,我也离开家乡去读大学。大伙都知道我是马里斯的头号球迷,便说:"你说你认识罗杰·马里斯,那就来证实一下吧。"于是我们一行六人驱车来到匹兹堡观看红雀队迎战海盗队的比赛,我清楚地记得那天是1967年5月9日。那是我第一次在洋基球场外看到身穿9号队服的马里斯。我心想,在这儿他不一定会认出我。当时我紧张极了,因为身边还站着五个同学,他要是真的认不出我,我就丢死人了。我走到围栏那儿,颤抖地叫道:"嗨,罗杰。"

他转了过来,说:"安迪,你怎么会在匹兹堡?"

那是我第一次知道他竟然还知道我的名字。"噢,罗杰,这些伙伴都是我学校的,他们想来见你,我也就顺便过来问候你一下。"五个伙伴一个挨着一个和罗杰握了手,都不敢相信这会是真的。我祝罗杰好运!然后他说:"等会儿,送你一颗我签名的联赛棒球。"他走到休息区,拿来一颗球,并在上面签了名。我接过球,感觉好像拿着100万大钞。

现在,想起这些,自己都觉得是种享受。我想,在球迷与球星之间,尤其在孩子和他们心中的偶像之间,一定存在着某种特殊的关系,或者可以说是存在着某种奇迹。就像那一次我和其他五个伙伴儿一起到匹兹堡看罗杰时,现在想来一切都还历历在目,而当时却像做梦一样。

那天我经历了生命中的一个奇迹。那是罗杰在联赛上的第一个本垒打,而我就在那刻得到了那颗球。激动的泪水顺着我的脸颊流下。罗杰在那局结束时跑过来对我说:"我简直不能相信这是真的。"我说:"你不相信?我也一样!"

5月9日——我唯一去球场观看的一天,9号队员的本垒打球击中了坐在右场9排9座的我,这样的机会是多么的渺小啊!我只能说这是个奇迹——一个在球迷和他的偶像之间发生的美妙的奇迹!

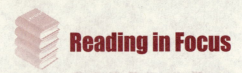

## Reading in Focus

语篇中概括句的识别 Recognize the Concluding Sentences

I. Direction: You are asked to identify the conclusion sentences of the following passages by using the reading skill mentioned above.

1. 主语(带有定语从句)  2. 介词宾语(带有定语从句)  3. 表语(带有定语从句)
4. 宾语(带有定语从句)  5. 宾语(从句)  6. 介词宾语(从句)
7. 主语(带有定语从句)  8. 表语(带有定语从句)

II. Direction: Try to find out the conclusion sentences in the Text A and B, and see how these sentences improve your understanding of the texts.

# Keys to Test Three

**Tape scripts for Listening Comprehension**
**Part I Listening Comprehension**
**Section A (12 points)**

1. M: May I smoke here?
   W: No, smoking will harm the patients.
   Q: Where do you think the conversation probably takes place?

2. M: Oh, no. It's 5:30 already, and I haven't finished typing these letters.
   W: Don't worry. That clock is half an hour fast. You still have time to do them.
   Q: When did this dialogue take place?

3. W: Excuse me, Mr. Smith. Can I borrow these books? I need them for my chemistry course.
   M: Sorry. You are not allowed to have more than five books out at a time.
   Q: Who is Mr. Smith?

4. W: Would you like to have something else to eat, sir?
   M: No, thank you. Just bring me the bill please.
   Q: What is the relationship between the two speakers?

5. W: Did you see the late movie on TV last night?
   M: No. I intended to, but fell asleep.
   Q: Why did the man miss the TV program?

6. M: How do you compare this apartment with the one we saw last week?
   W: I prefer this one. It has one more room.
   Q: What do we learn from this conversation?

7. M: Do you mind if I take a look at your book?
   W: No, not at all. It's on the desk.
   Q: What does the woman mean?

8. W: What do you think of Tom's presentation?
   M: It was interesting, but he was not very at ease in front of the class.
   Q: What does the man say about Tom?

9. M: I heard that the show in the city is very popular.
   W: I'd like to go, but there are only a few seats left.
   Q: What does the woman imply?

10. W: Want to go for a bike ride or fishing?
    M: You're not going to do your experiment, are you?
    Q: What does the man mean?

11. M: Good morning. My name is John Brown and I have an account with your company.
    W: Sorry. I didn't catch your name.
    Q: What most probably will the man do in response to the woman's words?

12. W: Hi, Jim! I thought you were going to that meeting in London.
    M: It was called off just as I was about to leave for the airport.
    Q: What happened to Jim?

### Section B (10 points)

Faces, like fingerprints, are unique. Did you ever wonder how it is possible for us to recognize people? Even a skilled writer probably could not describe all the features that make one face different from another. Yet a very young child—or even an animal, such as a pigeon—can learn to recognize faces. We all take this ability for granted. We also tell people apart by how they behave. When we talk about someone's personality, we mean the ways in which he or she acts, speaks, thinks and feels that make that individual different from others. Like the human face, human personality is very complex. But describing someone's personality in words is somewhat easier than describing his face. If you were asked to describe what a "nice face" looked like, you probably would have a difficult time doing so. But if you were asked to describe a "nice person," you might begin to think about someone who was kind, considerate, friendly, warm, and so forth. There are many words to describe how a person thinks, feels and acts. An American psychologist found that nearly 18,000 English words are used to describe differences in people's behavior. And people have always tried to "type" each other. Actors in early Greek drama wore masks to show the audience whether they played the villain's (坏人) or the hero's role. In fact, the words "person" and "personality" come from Latin, meaning "mask". Today, most television and movie actors do not wear masks. But we can easily tell the "good guys" from the "bad guys" because the two types differ in appearance as well as in actions.

### Part I Listening Comprehension
**Section A (12 points)**
1. C  2. B  3. A  4. D  5. B  6. C  7. D  8. A  9. B  10. B  11. A  12. D

## Section B (10 points)

1. wonder    2. describe    3. granted    4. behave
5. acts    6. complex    7. somewhat    8. friendly
9. people have always tried to "type" each other
10. most television and movie actors do not wear masks
11. because the two types differ in appearance as well as in actions

## Part II Reading Comprehension (30 points)

1-5 BCADB    6-10 CABDB    11-15 DCBCD    16-20 CADCD

## Part III Vocabulary & Structure (12 points)

1-5 ABACB    6-10 CDDBA    11-15 BABDC    16-20 BCABA    21-24 CDDB

## Part IV Cloze (10 points)

1-5 BDBCA    6-10 BACDC    11-15 ADCBA    16-20 ABDCA

## Part V Translation
### Section A (10 points)

1. 这些孩子们的年龄在 8 岁到 15 岁之间。
2. 我们将尽力赶超发达国家。
3. 我有一种坠落的感觉,像在梦中似的。
4. 到这个时候,我不在乎你决定要怎么做了。
5. 每一方有 12 名队员,还有主裁判和副裁判共两名裁判员。

### Section B (10 points)

**Direction: Translate the following sentences into English, using the words or phrases in the brackets.**

1. when he started out as a doctor
2. A host of friends met him at the railway station
3. allow him to stay out late
4. he would be involved in serious trouble
5. to acquaint the public with the fact

## Part VI Organizing Your Ideas (6 points)

c  f  d  b  a  e